START YOUR OWN
LAVENDER
BUSINESS

2 in 1 guide
growing and selling lavender for profit
+100 crafts, handmade gifts and natural remedies

DEMETER GUIDES

First edition: June 2021.

Published by DEMETER GUIDES

TABLE OF CONTENTS

INTRODUCTION
ABOUT LAVENDER

Known and used by mankind for more than 2,000 years, lavender has been primarily used since ancient times to perfume gardens and indoor environments thanks to its intense and inebriating fragrance, which also has a refreshing and relaxing effect.

The name of this plant originates from the Latin word "lavare" (to wash). It refers to the use that people, such as Greeks and Romans, made of it. They used to pick its flowers to perfume the water of the baths in which they immersed themselves, indulging in relaxing and soothing baths for the nerves and mind, but not only. Lavender was already used in those times as a base for refined perfumes and the creation of decoctions and infusions for the beauty of the skin and hair. The Egyptians were indeed the first to make archaic alembics to extract the essential oil of lavender, which they used in the delicate process of mummification. In this regard, when archaeologists first opened the tomb of Tutankhamen, they found, among the various herbs used to perfume the pharaoh, some residues of lavender flowers.

Although lavender has a history with origins dating to a very distant past, its place of birth remains a mystery. Even though it seems to come from Arabia or North Africa, there is no specific information about its precise origin. However, Pliny the Elder was the first to write about it in his works, describing it as one of the most used healing herbs around that time.

In the Middle Ages, a medicine used for intestinal cramps, nausea, vomiting, and hiccups was prepared with lavender. At the same period, on St. John's night - the summer solstice - were gathered the herbs of the field, including lavender, with which small bunches were formed, then used by young brides to perfume their trousseau and preserve linen from the danger of moths, leaving a pleasant scent on it.

During the Elizabethan period, in the second half of the 1500s, lavender had a first, lucky approach in the field of perfumery, giving life to the famous English perfume "The Lavender."

In more recent times, in the XX century, René-Maurice Gattefossé, the father of modern aromatherapy, began his studies on essential oils, starting from lavender flowers. In his 1937 book *Aromathérapie*, Gattefossé tells how, following a burn on his hand, he had the intuition to treat the wound with lavender oil, and, being amazed by the rapidity with which the burn healed, he began to analyze not only lavender but also many other medicinal plants, studying their therapeutic properties.

BENEFITS OF LAVENDER

Lavender easily lends itself to a thousand uses due to its beneficial properties. This plant, belonging to the family of Lamiaceae, can be used against headaches, coughs, insect stings, and the malaise of insomnia. Today, few plants in the world tantalize the senses the way lavender does. Nowadays, lavender and its essential oil are used in many fields, from cosmetics to nutrition, nutraceuticals, aromatherapy, phytotherapy, and pharmacology.

An essential oil can be obtained with lavender. In the inflorescence, we can find bracts, the persistent and colored leaves from which the flower develops, arranged in an opposite and spiral way. The number of flowers varies from two to ten. From these flowers, it is possible to extract an oil with several therapeutic properties:

- ✓ antidepressant
- ✓ antimicrobial
- ✓ anti-inflammatory
- ✓ healing
- ✓ relaxing

Lavender flowers can be employed to make scented sachets to put in linens or compositions, to both decorate and scent the room, thanks to its very characteristic violet color. Steam distillation of lavender creates a dense and yellow liquid with an intense odor. This oil represents a powerful ally against anxiety, depression, insomnia, irritability, headaches, and migraines. In some cases, it is also used to calm asthma, if related to the nervous system. Against infectious pathologies affecting the respiratory system, lavender provides an expectorant and fluidifying action. For this reason, it can be used to fight coughs, bronchitis, and laryngitis.

The essential oil of lavender is strongly antiseptic and calming, even for colic, and suitable for eliminating gas and intestinal swellings by attenuating the sensation of nausea and gastric reflux caused by indigestion. All in all, lavender is a plant with a thousand uses. In the garden, it is perfect for keeping away annoying and harmful insects while attracting pollinating bees. With lavender oil, it is possible to obtain lotions capable of relieving insect stings on the skin. It is an excellent first-aid remedy for its healing and antiseptic properties for stings, burns, wounds, and sores.

Moreover, thanks to the action on the central nervous system carried out by the volatile molecules contained in the essential oil, it is particularly suitable to treat states of restlessness and sleep disorders. It is also easy to find it useful for this purpose in sedative and relaxing herbal teas added to other plants, such as valerian, passionflower, chamomile, and lemon balm; but also, more simply in common and practical herbal pillows to be placed over the eyes and relax, or as a spray to be vaporized on the bed linen. Overall, it offers a total beneficial effect that involves all the senses.

THE MOST POPULAR TYPES OF LAVENDER

Lavender comes in a wide range of sizes and blooms. Likewise, the fragrance of the different lavender plants varies from type to type, just like the taste of good wine. Lavender is a perennial and evergreen plant growing in the Mediterranean basin. It has silvery leaves, also very scented, with a narrow and elongated shape. It is in high summertime that it produces many flowers, small and fragrant, grouped in spikes. Most varieties are resistant to cold and used in the garden as hedges or to form wide bushes.

Lavender roots are mainly woody, whereas the stems are usually erect and branched or simple, and the leaves ashy green. The lamina can be entire and linear, lanceolate or pinnatifida. The inflorescences are terminal, with the flowers grouped in thin spikes tyrsoid at the end of long scapes. The drug, which is the part of the plant that contains the active principles, is made of the flowering tops, which are harvested with the whole stem after fading, the moment at which the plant is richer in aromatic substances.

It is a rustic plant capable of resisting the most torrid summer heat and the most severe winters. In general, Lavandula angustifolia varieties tend to possess a more distinctive floral note. Consequently, oil from this species is found in high-end cosmetics and perfumes. These shrubs are dense and branched like stems, and the leaves are covered in a fine down that gives the whole thing a silvery appearance. This variety can reach up to five feet in height and prefers calcareous, well-drained soil. In this category belongs the dwarf lavender, also known as blue Hidcote, which is highly demanded for its compact aspect, adaptability, and abundance of flowers during the season.

However, the most common lavender in gardens is the grey edge, a variety of lavender x intermedia, a hybrid between Lavandula angustifolia and broadleaf. It is habitually medium to large-sized and very vigorous. It is the most used variety for the production of essences and the one cultivated in the south of France, where it is commonly called "lavandin." Very scented and robust, it is very common because it is very vigorous and has the advantage of quickly creating hedges. However, it is equally true that it soon tends to become very woody at the base, and therefore, rather unsightly. Another famous type of lavender is Lavandula stoechas, native to the Mediterranean basin and the Tyrrhenian lands. Lavandula stoechas contains a high amount of ketones, making it particularly pungent, very similar to rosemary. The main factors influencing fragrance are the soil, age of the plant, harvesting time, and rainfall levels.

For convenience, we tend to simplify plants' scientific names to avoid long, difficult-to-pronounce botanical names. Lavender has taken on many simplified names, so much so that various names are found in circulation, from English lavender to French lavender, and so on.

In the United States, Lavandula stoechas is often referred to as Spanish lavender, while in the United Kingdom, it is commonly referred to as French lavender.

ABOUT THIS GUIDE

Countless people stop on a hot summer day to stare in wonder at a lavender plant in full bloom. As the fragrance wafts up to their noses, they notice the beautiful color surrounding the flowering plant and all the bees moving from bud to bud, searching for pollen. If standing still long enough, the faint buzzing of these pollinators will mesmerize the senses into an overload of beauty. Lavender is a flower that is also and above all loved for this reason. By simply standing in the garden watering a flowering lavender plant, its scent and beauty are capable of dropping anyone into a satisfying trance state. Some people maintain this state of calmness for the next few minutes without getting such an experience out of their minds.

Having the opportunity to grow lavender is a privilege because it allows you to get in touch with nature and its times and riches, first and foremost, the beauty of lavender flowers. Spending time cultivating lavender is both a pleasure for the body and mind and a very profitable job. The demand for organic and natural goods is now very high and can be perfectly integrated into online blogs, social networks, and marketplaces dedicated to natural products. Growing lavender can become a full-time job for anyone passionate about agriculture and flowers and who wants to experience a new kind of economy: one that involves the total and extraordinary beauty of nature. If you are one of these people, have questions about how to make your lavender look its best and grow thriving and healthy, or want to learn all about pruning, spacing and planting requirements, soil, irrigation, location, and more, this guide was made for you.

The cultivation of lavender can be of interest to different people with different purposes, from those who already have a farm and want to diversify their production and integrate income, to those considering starting a new business to make an income, to those who simply want to experiment with cultivation in an amateur and "hobbyist" way — maybe because they have an unused land. Depending on your purpose and starting situation, both the time commitment to devote to the activity and the investment will vary. This is an excellent way to ensure that the firm can count on potential partners in the project. We will identify the most appropriate varieties of lavender (mainly, as we shall see, officinal or hybrid), the extent of cultivation, machinery, equipment, necessary collaborators, etc., based on the quantity and type of products and services offered, and the kind of clientele.

The farmer will gain significant benefits from growing lavender using the organic farming method. Due to climate change and the considerable increase of the so-called conscious consumers, many people are looking not only for food, but also for personal hygiene, cosmetics, personal care, home care, genuine and safe, zero-kilometer, seasonal, and unharmful products for the environment. The organic farming of lavender is positioned in this interesting gap. Starting organic cultivation can open to the entrepreneur a further outlet on what, today, is undoubtedly a solid and fast-growing market. Regarding the location, the person who intends to start the cultivation is likely to already own a piece of land, and therefore, insert the activity in an already established farm.

In both cases, we must evaluate the presence of direct competitors in the chosen area and the potentiality of the market, for example, by inquiring about the existence of consortia and producers' associations, which can take care of picking up the productions.

To limit the investment and test the market, we believe it is preferable to start with a small production and a few types of machinery, maybe bought used. If the products are appreciated and the activity works well, you can later expand the range of products offered, indulge in ideas, and buy more professional and sophisticated machinery, allowing you to increase your production and save time and effort.

The owner of the activity must also keep up with the various aspects related to the cultivation of the plant, the evolution of its market, and the latest technological innovations by participating in major trade fairs, keeping in touch with trade associations, and periodically consulting specialized websites and magazines.

Our suggestions also extend to advice on how to use lavender in daily life, and especially, how to open a business and start an activity entirely dedicated to lavender; how to succeed in selling and positioning yourself online; how the market of sustainability functions, what the target to intercept is; along with valuable tips on how to find the best products to sell them; how to propose them; and how to involve people in your lavender cultivation through unique experiences inside, workshops, and much more. The goal of this guide is to be comprehensive, and at the same time, allow you to become a part of a win-win business for the farmer, the consumer, and most importantly, the environment.

CHAPTER 1:
BEST LAVENDER TYPES

At this point, we are ready to start and go into more details about lavender cultivation. We have already discussed its history, benefits, uses, and why it is a profitable market. Here, we will introduce you to different types of lavender cultivation that vary in size, color, and fragrance. Each one has its own charm, and for each variety, we will describe its origin, the color of its flowers, length of the stems, conformation of the bush, and frequency of flowering. We will indicate the spacing, height, and robustness of the plant. It is essential to keep in mind that some varieties of lavender are protected by a patent, which means that their propagation for commercial use by anyone who is not a licensed grower is prohibited by the law. Remember that each plant has unique qualities and the colors are different in both flowers and foliage.

1. LAVANDULA ANGUSTIFOLIA

Under the designation, Lavandula angustifolia is considered the most cold-hardy species. Lavender plants are cultivated globally and in all climates for the precious essential oil they produce and their beauty in the garden. This type of lavender generally has a much sweeter smell than other species and is an excellent choice for culinary use. Aesthetically, the color spectrum of the bloom among the can include:

> - All shades of blue
> - Purple, from the lightest and faintest of flowers to the brightest purple through the periwinkle
> - Pink
> - White

The average Lavandula angustifolia plant measures 2 ½ feet, with stems reaching up to 13 inches. There are also smaller or dwarf varieties that are perfect for pots, while others can grow much larger, making them good for setting borders or a hedge.

The flowers of Lavandula angustifolia tend to be more vibrant than those of other species. Common lavenders should be planted in areas where they can be sheltered during the winter, while in areas with high rainfall, the owner must be careful with the soil and its drainage. On the one hand, lavender can benefit from the snow, which acts as an insulator. On the other hand, it can wither because of warm yet too humid places. The botanical term used to describe the stem that sprouts from the foliage and ends where the lavender flowers begin is the stalk. The stalk can grow more upright or have a wavy appearance. Lavenders can bloom once, twice, or more in a season, depending on how long the summer lasts and how early the flowers are picked. Thus, areas with warmer climates may have longer seasons and more blooms in a season due to the weather. The lavenders listed here bloom from early spring, including the first part of May, through early summer.

Three of the best-known varieties include:
- the Betty's Blue, Buena Vista, Royal Velvet, and Melissa, all native to Oregon, USA
- the Folgate and Royal Purple, coming from Norfolk, UK.

2. LAVANDULA XCHAYTORAE

Lavandula Xchaytorae is one of the largest varieties of lavender, making it perfect for decorating gardens. It has silvery leaves that remain healthy and strong even in the winter, allowing you to have thick, well-groomed, and beautiful hedges even in cold weather. Lavandula Xchaytorae is a variety of lavender that is hardy enough to survive harsh winters with temperatures below 5°F. When in bloom, it gives off a sweet and delicate scent and flowers, along with every available space of the shrub, and is perfect for creating lavender wands.

This lavender plant comes from a cross between Lavandula Lanata and Lavandula angustifolia.
Some of the most popular uses for this type of lavender include:
- the creation of hedges and flower beds
- the cultivation in planters or pots to embellish home corners.

It mainly blooms between June and July and reaches an average height of 27 inches. It prefers dry and well-drained soils and must be able to moderately take sunlight during the day. Although it does not have specific uses in cooking, it is one of the most suitable varieties of lavender to embellish with its beauty, gardens, and nurseries.

Among the most known varieties of Lavandula Xchaytorae, we can find:

- the Joan Head and Ana Luisa, the most common and well-known varieties of this type of lavender
- the Richard Grey, created in the royal botanical garden of London
- the Silver Frost, suitable for creating landscapes of unparalleled beauty.

3.   LAVANDULA × ALLARDII

Native to the Mediterranean, the Lavandula Xallardii is an attractive choice to enhance gardens with its combination of silver leaves and soft purple flowers. Perfect for temperate climates, it does not tolerate harsh winters, which is why you cannot cultivate it, except in greenhouses, where temperatures fall below freezing temperature.
It blooms during summer in a wonderfully delicate and whole way.

This variety of lavender was created by crossing lavender dentata with Lavandula latifolia. Its gray-green leaves are characteristic of this species, which reaches the largest size, erects habit, and vigorous growth.

The purple-colored inflorescence is elongated and thin, and the flowering is continuous between May and October.
It is a plant that tolerates heat well, and its preferred soil is the well-drained and dry soil of South Africa, France, and Australia.

4.   LAVANDULA DENTATA (fringed lavender or French lavender)

Named after its toothed leaves, it is also known as spikenard. This species is more delicate and tender, and for this reason, it should be planted somewhere where it can be protected during wintertime.
It is an excellent choice for pots and planters, and its fragrance is very reminiscent of eucalyptus.

Belonging to this family, for example, is Linda Ligon, which has light-colored foliage and purple inflorescences tending to pink. It is a delicate plant, even in its appearance, particular and unique.

The flowering of Lavandula dentata is very long, and in countries with a warm climate, blooms practically all year round.

5.   LAVANDULA × GINGINSII

This plant is actually a hybrid between Lavandula dentata and Lavandula Lanata (woolly lavender). The only known selection that has made it to date is the Goodwin Creek, which produces silvery-gray woolly foliage and thrives in warmer climates. This tender lavender should be protected during the winter. The leaves are not only toothed but irregular, and the flowers have a beautiful purple color and give this plant a bushy shape. It blooms from May to October if the climate allows it. At its full development, it can exceed 23 inches in height and a little more in width. Densely branched, this lavender has a well-lignified base and numerous stems, which, by dividing repeatedly and assuming an erect or slightly outwardly divided course, give the plant a rounded and compact shape. It prefers sunny or well-luminous positions, maybe with poor, dry, sandy, and above all, well-drained and permeable soils. It even tolerates prolonged periods of drought and adapts to saltiness in the sea winds of coastal locations.

6.   LAVANDULA × INTERMEDIA or lavandin

Lavandula × intermedia, or lavandins, is a cross between Lavandula angustifolia and Lavandula latifolia (pin lavender). This plant, which grows larger and blooms later, produces a good amount of more conspicuous spikes than other lavenders. The fragrance of the x intermedia lavender flowers has a characteristic camphoric note, which means that the extracted oil will have a woody undertone. Lavandins are primarily the most distilled lavenders because their oil yield can be up to five times that of the Lavandula angustifolia. They are perfect for creating a beautiful garden display and are an excellent choice for ground cover as they can over 48 inches tall and produce spikes up to 30 inches long. The colors are vibrant, and its best-known and most widely used variety is the Grosso, which possesses an intense fragrance and gray-green foliage and is particularly suited to compact, neat hedges. Its flowering lasts until August, and it can be very well be planted in a rocky garden.

In this category belongs the Alba lavender, with beautiful creamy white flowers, as well as the Edelweiss, also known as Grosso Bianca, because its gait is very similar, although its flowers are muffled. The Lavandula x intermedia, also called Fat Spike, is a good choice for creating scented wands and bags, fragrant memories with finer and longer spikes that are perfect for hedges, Fred Boutin of Californian origin, or Super of French origin. It is mainly used for the production of oil, and Impress purple, which represents the most suitable choice for the creation of a bouquet.

7. LAVANDULA MULTIFIDA

Lavandula Multifida is commonly referred to as fern leaf lavender and is also called Pubescens in the nursery industry. The ferny foliage makes it a lovely plant for small pots. However, its fragrance is among the least appealing ones. Indeed, some claim it smells like burnt rubber. It is also known as Egyptian lavender and is native to the southern regions of the Mediterranean sea, including Iberia, Sicily, and the Canary Islands.

The stem appears gray and woolly. The leaves are double-feathered, and the flowers are dark blue or blue-purple colored. Each flower has a stem above a leaf. This variety of lavender is grown both for medicinal purposes and as an ornamental plant. In colder latitudes, it is killed by winter frost, but it can be grown as a seasonal plant. This is one of the strangest lavenders around. Aesthetically particular, it is almost unrecognizable as true lavender. It is an elementary plant to grow that often reseeds itself.

8. LAVANDULA STOECHAS

Lavandula Stoechas is easily identified by its cylindrical heads wrapped around tiny flowers, topped with leaf-like extensions called bracts that look like rabbit ears or butterfly wings. The name of the species comes from the word *stoechades*, the ancient name of the group of islands off the French coast, now known as Îles d'Hyères, where the species is widespread. Also known as wild lavender or stecade, this beautiful plant can reach 15-25 inches, and exceptionally, even up to 4 feet. Its leaves are greyish due to the thick tomentose, with not thick but densely leafy ramification and an erect posture.

The plant is aromatic and is mainly used for its oil within the herbal sector. Moreover, lavender Stoechas produces an essential oil containing linalool and linalyl acetate and has precious antiseptic, mildly expectorant, and antispasmodic properties.

In the garden, wild lavender can be used to create a Mediterranean atmosphere in mixed forms, to which it can give a special spectacularity because of the abundant flowering and the intensity of the colors of its inflorescences. In the beekeeping sector, wild lavender is a charming melliferous plant. Honey obtained from this plant tastes clearly different from Lavandula angustifolia honey as it has a finer taste and is not very aromatic.

Its spontaneous flowering takes place many times during summertime. For this reason, this plant requires more frequent pruning. However, lavender Stoechas reseeds itself and is suited for rather high temperatures. In this category also belong the Ballerina varieties with purple flower heads and cream-colored buds. The upper bracts resemble the arms of a ballerina stretched in a bow above the head.

The Cottage Rose is among the most striking variety, with its dark fuchsia flowers and beautiful light pink upper bracts, and is ideal for adding a bit of variation to the garden. The Helmsdale also has an intense dark fuchsia color and is perfect for creating striking bushes. Although, the most unique variety is the James Compton, also sold as the Butterfly, which has a very unusual appearance with inflorescences that rise to the sky like a butterfly's wings. Finally, the Winter Bee comes from Australia and is among the first to bloom in the spring, and the Van Gogh is the greenest one and has lilac flowers coming from New Zealand.

9.   LAVANDULA VIRIDIS

It is among the most recognizable lavenders for its light green color and its white flower heads ringed with yellow and whitish-green bracts. It resists freezing temperatures for a short time and has an unusual smell, which reminds many citrus fruits, especially lemons. Native to southwestern Spain and southern Portugal, its stem reaches up to 8 inches and the yellow flower heads soon tend to turn brown.

10.   LAVANDULA LANATA

Known as lavender Lanata, this is a dwarf lavender native to southern Spain. It can only reach one meter in height and width and is particularly beautiful for the woolly, silvery hairs that grow pronounced on the leaves. The flowers are deep purple and give off a familiar scent. Developed primarily for its pleasing appearance and relaxing aroma, it also tolerates low temperatures down to 23°F but prefers, like all lavenders, a sunny location. Lavandula Lanata is perfect for keeping in terracotta pots and giving that rustic touch that only lavender possesses.

Best lavenders for Humid summers

These lavenders can withstand hotter, More humid temperatures in the summertime.

Lavandula ×chaytorae 'Ana Luisa'
L. ×chaytorae 'Kathleen Elizabeth'
L. ×intermedia 'Grosso'
L. ×intermedia 'Provence'
L. stoechas 'Otto Quast'

Best Cold-Weather Lavenders

These varieties have been proven to withstand colder temperatures and come back year after year.

Lavandula angustifolia 'Buena Vista'
L. angustifolia 'Folgate'
L. angustifolia 'Imperial Gem'
L. angustifolia 'Maillette'
L. angustifolia 'Royal Velvet'

All-Season Bloomers

For lavender that blooms more than once in a season.

Lavandula angustifolia 'Buena Vista'
L. angustifolia 'Croxton's Wild'
L. angustifolia 'French Fields'
L. angustifolia 'Sharon Roberts'
L. stoechas 'Madrid Purple'
L. stoechas 'Spanish Curly Top'

Lavenders with the Strongest Scent

These lavenders are known for their high oil content and strong fragrance. There are fragrant *Lavandula angustifolia* varieties, but they normally have a more delicate, floral note.

Lavandula ×intermedia 'Fat Spike'
L. ×intermedia 'Grosso'
L. ×intermedia 'Hidcote Giant'
L. ×intermedia 'Impress Purple'
L. ×intermedia 'Provence'
L. ×intermedia 'Super'

Ideal Lavenders by Bloom Color

If you want lavenders with dark blue, pink blossoms or richest purple, these types are excellent choices.

Darkest blues

L. angustifolia 'Betty's Blue'
L. angustifolia 'Blue Cushion'
L. angustifolia 'Thumbelina Leigh'
L. angustifolia 'Violet Intrigue'

Favorite pinks

L. angustifolia 'Coconut Ice'
L. angustifolia 'Hidcote Pink'
L. angustifolia 'Little Lottie'
L. angustifolia 'Melissa'
L. angustifolia 'Miss Katherine'

Richest purples

Lavandula angustifolia 'Hidcote'
L. angustifolia 'Hidcote Superior'
L. angustifolia 'Imperial Gem'
L. angustifolia 'Purple Bouquet'
L. ×intermedia 'Impress Purple'

CHAPTER 2:
HOW TO GROW LAVENDER

In many cases, if you decide to undertake the cultivation of lavender, you either already own a farm, such as an orchard, a medicinal and aromatic plant cultivation or a vegetable garden, or own a piece of land, perhaps uncultivated, and decided to experiment with cultivation, even as a hobby. The cultivation of land is a practice that requires discipline, attention, and reflection. For this reason, it is a hobby that many have resumed to slow down from the frenetic modern life and assume new rhythms marked by nature. Plants are a constant reminder of the cycle of life and rebirth, and growing lavender is immensely relaxing and will help you rediscover the beauty of contact with the earth. Starting a business or start-up dedicated to organic lavender cultivation is a sage and profitable choice. In many countries, there are often incentives for this type of activity that enhance the territory and feed a natural business in full respect of biodiversity. It is enough to go to the competent offices of one's region to know how to access this new type of activity.

The cultivation of lavender is a more flexible activity than one may think and allows the entrepreneur to decide autonomously how to set up their business and to which kind of sale to dedicate themselves. This decision depends on many factors, including the hours dedicated to the actual activity. However, it should be noted that for the specific processing and transformation of officinal plants, there are legal requirements both for the certification of the raw material, such as the use in cosmetic products, and in terms of required qualifications.

Therefore, you must inquire about this at the trade associations and the competent offices of the region/state/country of reference.
It is possible to create different business formats for the lavender farm, such as the cultivation and sale of raw materials only, the cultivation and distillation of the raw material, or the cultivation with a processing laboratory.

The cultivation and sale of raw material only could refer to cultivation that is already underway and aspires to diversify its activity and integrate its income by allocating part of the available land to the cultivation of lavender. Therefore, the owner could decide to cultivate limited quantities of this plant, in not particularly vast areas, instead focusing on the high quality of the products. In this case, it is possible to sell only the raw material without processing it on-site, at consortia, associations of producers, or processing companies in the area, which will therefore be the primary customer segment. As for the species of lavender to be cultivated, it is good to choose one according to the customer demand in the area. Investments for cultivating lavender in an existing farm are more limited. Of course, at a later time, it will be possible to choose to enlarge the area cultivated with lavender and to do some processing, in case sales are remarkably positive and the demand for the catchment area increases.

Another case is that of a company that, besides cultivation, also distills the raw material. This format includes the possibility of distilling the raw material on the spot. Suppose it is decided to transform lavender flowers first and distill them to obtain the precious essential oil. In that case, you must set up a small laboratory near the farm. However, there may already be an area destined for the processing and transformation of the raw material produced, in case of an already established farm.

As this cultivation also carries out the distillation of lavender flowers, it would be preferable to choose to plant a particularly productive species under this point of view, such as lavandin, which can produce more essential oil than its counterparts. Moreover, in this case, compared to the previous one, you will have to rely on higher human resources and higher availability in terms of time and investments. On the other hand, producing lavender's essential oil opens to the owner of the cultivation of new influential outlets on the market, widening his potential customers, and therefore, his revenues.

A last opportunity is given through a cultivation and processing laboratory, an activity mainly dedicated to new companies. This allows them to start an innovative and more complete activity, which not only includes the cultivation but also the processing of the raw material into food, cosmetic, herbal products, and much more, with the wonderful base made of lavender. The product resulting from these cultivations can be sold in raw material to processors and the finished product to final consumers or stores. When cultivating with a processing workshop, the initial investment will naturally be higher than in the previous cases. However, the range of products offered can be significantly expanded and, consequently, bring about a wider and more heterogeneous clientele.

THE COMPOSITION OF THE LAND

Initially, it will be necessary to adapt the available soil to the cultivation of lavender. If the soil does not possess the ideal characteristics, it is possible to obtain a good product by adopting some precautions related to cultivation and fertilization. To better adapt the soil to the cultivation of lavender, it is fundamental to know its characteristics, determined by a series of compositional, physical, mechanical, chemical, and biological elements. It will allow the cultivation to grow luxuriantly and regenerate by drawing from the properties of the land itself. First of all, you must check the pH value of the soil and that of the water used for irrigation. If it is too alkaline, you will have to filter it.

Then, it will be possible to check the drainage capacity of the soil, a crucial factor for lavender's needs. A drainage test can be performed by digging a hole about 23 inches deep and 7-8 inches wide and filling it with water. Once the water has been absorbed, the hole must be refilled with water. At this point, if the soil takes less than 12 hours to drain the liquid, it has very good drainage. Meanwhile, if it takes 12 to 24 hours, it is a heavier and clayey soil, whereas, if it takes more than 24 hours, the soil is not at all suitable for the cultivation of lavender. Once you have evaluated the drainage capacity of the soil and its composition, you may, if necessary, make it more suitable for the optimal growth of lavender or lavandin.

To correct an excessively clayey soil which, as previously seen, is poorly tolerated by Lavandula, we start by loosening the area with a spade, to a depth of 10-15 inches. This area must be a little larger than the area you intend to cultivate. When the roots of the lavender or lavandin plants begin to expand, if they encroach on the clay soil, they will fold in on themselves to return to where the soil is better, causing problems to the root ball. Remember that the soil should preferably be tilled when dry. A very wet clayey soil is less compact, and therefore, makes the correction more difficult.

We, therefore, proceed by correcting the soil according to the result of the test. Most soils are alkaline, in which case, as we have previously seen, it will not be necessary to correct the pH, precisely because Lavandula grows well in this type of soil.

On the other hand, you will have to intervene if the soil is too acid by incorporating lime. This correction is generally applied to the soil before working and repeated every two or three years. In case you decide to start biological cultivation, the soil must meet other specific requirements. First of all, it cannot be near possible sources of pollution, such as fruit cultivations treated with pesticides, industries that discharge polluting gases or waters, etc.

In this regard, you must pay attention to irrigation waters, which can harm the final quality of the essential lavender oil if it is polluted by discharges upstream of the areas of use. At the same time, you have to check for the presence of heavy metals in the soil (such as lead, for example), which can alter the presence and effectiveness of the active principles of plants. Organic cultivation must maintain and enhance the life and natural fertility of the soil, its stability, and its biodiversity. It must also prevent and combat soil compaction and erosion and nourish plants mainly through the soil ecosystem. Organic farming, as such, has as its leading principle harmony with the natural system and the respect of biodiversity. In organic farming, it is therefore forbidden to use external chemical substances such as fertilizers, insecticides, herbicides, fungicides, pesticides, and drugs of any kind, as these would damage the fertility of the soil, the genuineness of the food, and would seriously endanger biodiversity. Another fundamental rule of organic farming is the total absence of GMOs (genetically modified organisms) to adhere to the same principle of safeguarding and respecting the natural ecosystem and our planet's biodiversity.

THE EXTENSION OF CULTIVATION

A choice contingent on the location of cultivation concerns the size of the activity and, consequently, the land surface available for cultivation. This decision is determined both by the size of the land available and one's objectives. Regardless of these, it is always preferable to start with trials in a limited area. At a later stage, you can continue cultivating a small space as a hobby or for supplementary income, or expand the site and production to give an entrepreneurial stamp to the activity and sell to individuals, stores, or processors. In any case, you must always provide the plants with enough space for proper growth by ensuring that they will not be moved. To get an idea of the extension needed for the realization of a lavender and lavandin cultivation, consider that, generally, the planting pattern of lavender cultivation foresees a distance between rows of 20-23 inches and a distance between plants of the same row of 3'2 to 3'7 (about two plants per 10 square feet).

For lavender, instead, the ideal distance between rows is 15 inches, and the distance between plants of the same row is 6'5. The obtainable productions vary a lot according to the species and the age of the plants (which produce from the third year up to about the tenth or twelfth year, with a peak at the sixth or seventh year). This production ranges from 1,780 up to a maximum of 6,260 lbs. per acre of flowers for lavender, and from 3,750 up to 13,150 lbs. per acre for lavandin. These figures are for fresh products. Meanwhile, the average yield of the dried product ranges from 713 to 1,070 lbs. per acre for officinal lavender, and from 900 to 1,785 lbs. per acre for lavandin. The yield in essential oil, starting from fresh products, is very variable, whereas, for lavender, it is approximately between 0.5% and 1.5%, and between 1% and 3% for lavandin. In other words, from 220 lbs. of fresh lavender flowers, we obtain between 1 and 3.3 lbs. of essential oil. 2.2 lbs. of essential oil corresponds to about 37 ounces.

THE PREPARATION OF THE SOIL

One cannot cultivate Lavandula without a good preparation of the soil. It must indeed be well-leveled, clean from weeds, and free of water stagnation. First of all, the soil must be milled at 3.9-4.7 inches, to break up the superficial crust and eliminate the unwanted vegetal cover. In this way, you will obtain very clean and friable soil. This operation, generally done by using a tiller or a motor cultivator with a tiller, can also be supported by green manure to provide first fertilization to the soil. Green manure is a practice that consists of burying specific crops to maintain or increase soil fertility in order to cultivate particular plants and bury the green mass-produced instead of removing it from the soil. The most used plant families for green manure are leguminous plants because they fix, with their root system, atmospheric nitrogen enriching the soil with nitrogen. Green manure must be done before sowing or planting lavender and lavandin cuttings and allows the producer to improve soil fertility and structure at very low costs.

In the fields, green manure is practiced with a plow, or with a spade in vegetable gardens or family-organized crops. Green manure aims to increase the properties and improving soil protection by:

✓ Decreasing the corrosive phenomenon
✓ Maintaining nitric nitrogen content
✓ Developing organic matter in the soil
✓ Fertilizing hot-arid soils, without needing to manure
✓ Perfecting the soil for organic farming.

Before fertilization, you must dig into the soil to a depth of about 15-20 inches. Depending on the extent of the soil, you can do so by hand, with a spade, or using a motor hoe.

During the digging, a first furrow is made for the whole length of the field and is destined to the plants of Lavandula. Then, the organic fertilizer, which must be well mature, is placed along this furrow using a fork. At this point, a second furrow is made, parallel to the first one, whose clods will cover the fertilizer placed in the first one. Then, the second furrow is filled with manure and covered with the third furrow's clods, continuing until the end of the field. The soil that will host lavender and lavandin plants must be fertilized with manure at a rate of about 15-22 tons/acre. Conventional fertilization for the cultivation of Lavandula consists of 45-53 lbs./acre of nitrogen (N), phosphorus (P2O5), and potassium (K20) at planting, followed by 53-62 lbs./acre of N, and K20 to be given in the following years, during spring tilling operations.

Once the fertilization and digging phase are over, the whole field must be leveled, breaking up the biggest clods. The soil is then left to rest until the moment of seeding or transplanting.

Finally, rows can be regularized and passageways deepened a fortnight after sowing or planting.

HOW TO PLANT LAVENDER

We can propagate the lavender plant through different methods, which cannot disregard the species of Lavandula one will choose to cultivate. While officinal lavender can be propagated by seed, a hybrid species, such as lavender, must be propagated by cuttings.

SEEDING

For propagation by seed, which can be done only with the Lavandula species found in nature, one must prepare the seedbeds in February/March or in the fall, because the seed, not very germinable, must be subjected to low temperatures (about 35°F for a week) or treated with gibberellic acid. Generally, we use about 0.07 oz of seed per 10 square feet, from which we obtain about 600 seedlings, which, once they develop at least two true leaves, are thinned to 1/sq ft., or transferred into single containers, with honeycombs. Seeds must be distributed in the seedbed so that they are covered by about 0.4 inches of moist soil. Water stagnation mustn't occur as it could cause the formation of fungi and kill young seedlings. After 60 to 70 days, we do the final transplanting, once the seedlings have reached a height of 4 inches. A 215-260-square-foot seedbed can provide the necessary plants for one acre of land.

TRANSPLANTING

Propagation by cuttings, which is possible for lavender plants and necessary for lavandin, is done in the fall or early spring, taking partially woody twigs from young mother plants of 2-3 years of life. Cuttings are nothing else than the fragment of a plant that is purposely cut and placed in the soil, or even in water, to regenerate the missing parts, thus giving life to a new specimen. Most of the time, it is a sprig destined to take root. This method takes advantage of the enormous regenerative properties of plants, capable of rebuilding themselves from a fragment of leaf, stem, or root. Each partially woody cutting must have a length of 4-5 inches and a diameter of 0.1-0.2 inches. The separation cut from the mother plant must be clean and always made under a node. The basal leaves must then be removed to avoid rottenness and reduce transpiration and should be buried 1-1.5 inches deep. Generally, the best cuttings are those obtained from lateral branches that have not flowered, detached with a part of old wood (the so-called heel), or leaving a piece of the original branch (knitting cuttings). To plant 2.5 acres of lavender garden, we need about 20,000 cuttings, usually taking into account 50% of failures. Generally, lavender cuttings are not directly planted, but in nurseries, in rows that are 15 inches apart and 6 inches on the row, and transplanted the following year. For one acre of lavender cultivation, we need about 345-390 square feet of nursery. Transplanting, an operation that can generally be mechanized, is done in the spring with rooted 1-year-old cuttings. Seedlings should be planted deep, with 3'2-6'6 m between rows and 1-2 feet on the row, depending on the species and cultivars used, as previously seen. Another solution is to buy Lavandula seedlings at nurseries or local growers, which can be initially grown in pots. Then, when temperatures rise above 59°F, they can be moved outdoors, in the previously prepared field, and keeping in mind the distances between plants. However, as lavender plants become fully productive when they are two or three years old, many growers prefer to start cultivating them by purchasing already mature plants and transplanting them into their own soil to obtain already productive plants.

When purchasing the plant, it is good to verify that it actually is the requested species of lavender, ask for the age of the shrub in order to know in advance what the productive expectation of the first year of planting will be, and inquire about the way the plant has been reproduced. Therefore, it is fundamental to rely on floriculturists or specialized nurseries, which can prove the origin of the plants with relevant certifications. Once purchased, plants should be planted at the end of fall to allow an excellent vegetative start in the spring. Before transferring the plant, you must make sure its roots are humid and, in case they are not wet enough, soak them for a short time in a bucket of lukewarm water. At this point, the plant can be transferred into a pot or the ground. If transplanted in the ground, the holes for planting must be made with wet soil, using a wooden awl to enter deeper into the ground. The hole will have to be big enough to completely contain the bread of soil where the roots and base of the plant are located. Once the plants have been transplanted, proceed with compacting the soil around the stems and with watering.

However, if the plant is to be planted in a pot to be ready in the spring, you should cover the bottom of the pot with a layer of expanded clay, which will favor a better keeping of humidity in the soil.

IRRIGATION OF LAVENDER

First of all, you must underline how irrigation parameters, including the dose and turn, must be calculated not only according to the specific needs of the Lavandula plant, but also the climate and water capacity of the soil. Environmental conditions are in fact peculiar and can cause very different reactions from one cultivation to another, caused mainly by some of the soil characteristics, such as the presence of sand, clay, or stones, to name a few.

That being said, lavender and lavandin do not have significant watering needs. As previously discussed, these plants do not like excessive humidity and can handle much less water stagnation in the soil, which can rot its roots. The frequency of watering must, therefore, be balanced and moderate. The method to distribute the correct quantity of water to the plant is to only water once the soil is completely dry. The same is true between irrigations: the next one must be done when the soil is perfectly dry. For lavender, the ideal water can also contain a certain amount of limestone, as this species is not at all a lover of acid soils and, on the contrary, likes alkaline soils that contain limestone or silicon. Of course, too much limestone could create basal deposits, which would prevent the plant from transpiring. It is therefore essential to carefully measure the quantity and quality of irrigations. Consequently, we suggest watering lavender daily, immediately after planting, and do more sporadic watering as the plant grows and its water needs decrease. It is possible to install a localized drip irrigation system, which permits you to administer water slowly but continuously and locally. As a result, it will enable the root system to absorb the right amount of water without it flowing to areas where it is not needed nor stagnating. Then, when the plant matures, at about four years of age, the fully developed root system will be able to supply itself in-depth, and the plant will need less water and a milder irrigation system. You will have to reduce watering to once or twice a week. At the same time, you should mulch the soil around the plants to keep it moist. Mulching can be done by covering the soil with a layer of material, including plastic film, but also sand or shredded bark, to prevent weed growth but also to:

> ➤ maintain moisture in the soil
> ➤ protect the soil from erosion and the action of heavy rain

> ➢ mitigate the soil temperature
> ➢ avoid the formation of the so-called superficial crust
> ➢ decrease compaction
> ➢ maintain the structure.

In pot cultivation, the plants will have slightly different needs than specimens grown in the ground. Therefore, you should pay more attention to water and nutritional needs, and check for the presence of parasites more often. It is advisable to proceed with regular watering, although never abundant, and choose a large pot with expanded clay to improve soil drainage.

WEEDING

Taking care of a plant also means knowing how to defend it from winter or attacks performed by small insects and bacteria, and above all, from weeds that do not allow the plant to proceed with a healthy life and that can affect its proper growth and flowering. Weeds do not have any valuable function for man, but they damage agricultural production and can therefore be one of the main cost factors. Particularly in the case of the cultivation of aromatic and officinal plants, weeds are the most frequent cause of product loss. High competitiveness does not characterize lavender species, thus making the competition with weeds, which are instead characterized by an intense aggressiveness, unequal. This type of flora proves to be very resistant and able to overpower the medicinal plant quickly. Destructive infestations especially occur in organic crops; they are particularly harmful in multi-year or perennial crops, such as lavender, often compromising their duration. To effectively fight against weeds, you could integrate the agronomic fight with the chemical one. Among the agronomic means, it is possible to:

1. Crop rotation, generally every six years. It prevents weeds from adapting and selecting since they are disturbed by different cultivations year after year;

2. Harrow and weed: the first is a light tilling that allows to refine the soil and control the emergence of weeds, while the second remixes the surface layer of the inter-row, thus mechanically destroying weeds, favoring the circulation of air in the soil, and facilitating the penetration of solar heat into the soil in cold climates;

3. False seed, a practice that consists of preparing the seedbed and irrigating it without burying the seeds. In this way, weeds will germinate before the crop is planted and can be removed by hand or by harrowing;

4. Mulch, which consists of covering the soil with organic or inorganic material to contrast the germination of weed seeds. It is one of the most effective and long-term solutions.

The fight against weeds can also include the use of pesticides, called herbicides, which are forbidden in organic farming. They can be weed killers (not to be used in presence of the crop),anti-sprout, and graminicides. The distribution of herbicides is a moment that requires the analysis of several factors, such as the stage of the crop, type of soil, distribution equipment, degree of the infestation, and others. A wrong evaluation can lead to the failure of such treatments.

CROP ROTATION

In the case of a farm that, in addition to lavender, also grows other plants, such as medicinal, aromatic, horticultural, cereal, and many different varieties and types, it is advisable to carry out a crop rotation every 5/6 years. Crop rotation is, in fact, an important technique, as it permits to keep the soil fertile, thus ensuring satisfactory productions, both in terms of quantity and quality. On the contrary, cultivating the same plant in the same plot for many years inevitably reduces the levels of soil fertility, does not interrupt the cycle of weeds, and, in many cases, does not counteract the onset of parasitic diseases. In a farm that also carries out lavender and lavandin cultivations, an optimal rotation can be done by alternating the various plots of land and the cultivation of plants belonging to different botanical families that have a different absorption of nutritional elements. Generally speaking, the succession should be done between plants that significantly exploit the soil without leaving residues and plants capable of enriching the soil with nutrients called ameliorative substances. In this way, the soil will always benefit from new substances able of growing future plants naturally and in a better way.

This operation can also be done by planting one or more intercropping grasses. To implement this technique, it is appropriate to draw up a crop rotation plan for each portion of cultivated land. Morcover, the use of leguminous plants allows the addition of symbiotic nitrogen to the soil. More generally, the composition of the various crop residues contributes to the quality of the humus.

Going into the merit of the lavender field, horticultural, cereal, or forage species, preferably belonging to different families, can be included in the plan. For example, a rotation model envisages planting a fall-winter cereal, such as spelt or pearl barley, in the first year. It is followed by sowing or planting lavender plants. At the end of the lavender plants' productive phase (fourth/fifth year), the rotation is completed with a multi-year row plant (such as the officinal sage, mint, or lemon balm).

PRUNING

Pruning is indispensable in order not to make lavender and lavandin age prematurely, making them immediately go, as they say in slang, "to wood." As for the period, lavender is pruned at the end of flowering. This plant blooms between spring and summer, and the exact time for the appearance of flower spikes always depends on the species cultivated. Pruning lavender consists of topping the apical shoots and shortening the stem. Both these methods favor the emission of new shoots and improve the plant's appearance and structure.

Flower stems can be cut more drastically. In other words, they can be further shortened if the plant is in danger of drying up or strongly debilitated by adverse external conditions. Also, tools for pruning lavender must be cleaned before and after each use.

Although not the only one, the best period for pruning lavender is after flowering. Experts suggest pruning twice a year, both after summer, between September and October, and after winter, between the end of February and the beginning of March. Double pruning allows, regardless of the variety of lavender, a higher and more profitable flowering. Pruning lavender is not a complicated operation, and even those who are not experts can do it without any problem by respecting some simple indications. First of all, it is necessary to have gardening scissors and a pair of gloves. Then, you can proceed as follows. For the right pruning, you need to cut off dry stems by making a clean cut about ¾ of an inch above the branches, at the base of the plant. After that, you must give the plant a clean-cut trying to give it a rounded shape and an aesthetically pleasing aspect. If the bush is small, a pair of scissors is enough, otherwise, you must use long-bladed shears for bigger and woody branches. Following the lavender pruning operation, you can keep taking care of your plant as usual, without observing any further precautions. Once the cut has been done, wounds must be swabbed to protect the plant from pests' assault. To tamponade the cuts, it is necessary to use proper healing mastic to close the wounds and act as a barrier to pests.

Pruning allows the plant to grow healthily and makes it more resistant to bad weather conditions. Moreover, it aims to favor aeration and illumination, which is ideal to obtain a constant and very high-quality product and a functional and aesthetical harmony between the foliage and the roots. Generally, to perform the best pruning of lavender, you must cut about two-thirds of the vegetation and remove the dry spikes. Ideally, you should leave at least four buds for each stem. Even though the plant will look pretty bare for a while, pruning is unavoidable and indispensable to ensure a lush and healthy growth. Also, you do not need to worry as it will soon return to its original, compact state. The substitution of the tuft can be done by planting a new lavender plant or by renewing it, which includes drastic pruning. If the plant is replaced, you will not need to uproot it without leaving the root part completely buried. To remove the whole root, dig a hole and fill it with fertile soil, if necessary. Lavender must never be pruned during the winter, especially if the plant is located in an area that experiences cold temperatures and frequent frosts.

GROWING LAVENDER AT HOME

Lavender is a plant that, while preferring wide open spaces, can also effectively grow in pots. Moreover, not everyone has a big enough and optimal soil for growing lavender or other plants. Still, by following some little tricks, you may grow lavender indoors and get excellent results that will be helpful because of the products obtained and will beautify the home environment. The first step to growing lavender and lavandin in a pot is to prepare the dwelling properly. On the pot, you will have to prepare a bottom of gravel and crocks or expanded clay balls to ensure a good water flow. Then, after placing the soil in the pot, and before sowing or potting, you should soften it in-depth, making it less compact so that the plant's roots can easily find space and branch properly. This operation can be done by hand or with the help of a small transplanter or hoe. When cultivating in pots, the soil will have to be changed every year, as Lavandula plants grow, develop, and feed on the available substances, "consuming" the soil. As for watering, it should be more abundant than the amount needed by a plant placed in the ground. However, you must always remember not to exaggerate in order not to let the plant's roots rot. Ideally, you should water about once a week in the winter. In contrast, between May and July, in full blooming, it is preferable to increase the number of weekly waterings to two-three, without abounding too much.

Between one watering and the other, it is good to let the soil of the pot dry to avoid the formation of stagnations and help the vegetative development of the plant. It is also possible to add liquid organic fertilizer to the water every 15-20 days. Toward the end of March, minor pruning will later ensure a greater flowering. The pot can be positioned in different locations, depending on the season and temperatures. During winter, pots with lavender or lavandin plants can be placed in a closed environment, such as a veranda or greenhouse, which will protect them from excessive cold, rain, and frosts. For small and medium-sized cultivations, the most suitable greenhouse is the so-called "tunnel greenhouse." It is an arch-shaped steel structure, usually of limited height, covered by a water-repellent PVC sheet provided with a filter for ultraviolet rays.

Instead, during the flowering phase, it is preferable to place the plants in the open air, favoring direct sun exposure for at least eight hours a day. In this way, it will provide higher-quality flowers.

This type of cultivation offers some advantages over the cultivation in the open ground.

1. First of all, growing Lavandula in a greenhouse can be useful, especially at the beginning, to test the feasibility and yield of the cultivation.
2. In addition, this method requires less space and labor than growing some in the ground, making it particularly suitable for those who choose to grow lavender or Lavandula as a hobby. However, just like the cultivation in the ground, the cultivation in a greenhouse requires specific procedures and tricks that can compromise the good yield of the lavender garden if not or poorly done.

THE BIOLOGICAL CYCLE OF LAVENDER

Lavandula, and every species belonging to this category, is a perennial plant capable of living several years, and that has a vegetative and a reproductive period each year. In the vegetative phase, which usually reflects the autumnal and spring periods, the plant roots take root to the ground and develop. Flowering, which marks the beginning of the reproductive phase, usually occurs between June and September, a period that varies according to the species, yearly climate, and geographical location of the cultivation. Generally, officinal lavender blooms between May and July, whereas lavandin blooms between June and August. It is during the flowering phase that the difference between lavender and lavandin becomes even more evident. In fact, while the flowering spike of lavender carries a single inflorescence, which can be from 1 to 1 ½ inch long, three branches depart from each the flowering spike of the lavandin.

At the end of the summer, once the flowering phase is over, the lavender plant enters a period of vegetative rest. However, as an evergreen plant, it does not assume the dry characteristic and withered aspect of resting plants. Still, it keeps its silvery-green color, as well as its leaves.

CHAPTER 3.
HOW TO HARVEST LAVENDER

On average, lavender cultivation comes into total production on its third year and remains productive until its tenth or twelfth year, after which it must be harvested. It usually peaks around its sixth or seventh year. The period of flowering changes according to the species and the pedoclimatic characteristics of the territory. It can take place from early June to early September. Likewise, the time suitable for harvesting changes according to the use made of the flowers. Lavender flowers, which are more precocious, are to be harvested at the beginning of flowering, between June and July if they are used in herbal medicine, and in August if they are used for distillation, in which case the whole spike with the seed is to be harvested. Even lavandin flowers will be harvested at the beginning of flowering for herbalist use. However, the beginning of flowering is delayed by one month compared to lavender, and it occurs between July and August. Instead, lavender flowers harvested for distillation will be harvested between August and September, when the flowers are fully bloomed. Therefore, the best time to harvest the product to be distilled is at the beginning of the flowering period, as the percentage of the essence and its main components do not change after the wilting of the flowers; in any case, when the plants are no longer foraged by bees. Instead, for the herbal product, harvesting is done at the beginning of flowering, either by hand, in medium and large-sized lavandin groves, or mechanically, by using harvesting machines (reapers) with a working capacity equal to 2 ½ acres of land in about three hours. The yield in inflorescences grows in the first 6-7 years of planting, reaching a maximum of 1 ½ - 2 ¼ oz/1075 sq. ft. for lavender and 4-5 oz/1075 sq. ft. for lavandin, then decreasing in the following years. The yield in herbal products (shelled flowers) is ¼ - ½ oz/100 sq. ft. for lavandin, and slightly less for lavender. Harvesting, however, should be done in favorable climatic conditions, with dry soil and no rain nor high humidity.

DRYING

Depending on the format chosen for your business, lavandin can handle the drying of the harvested lavender flowers directly. Drying or desiccating is a stabilization process that moves tissue water away from the stigma without changing its chemical composition, except for some highly volatile substances. This process also blocks enzymatic and microbial systems. You can dry lavender inflorescences naturally or artificially. Natural drying is done in the air — sometimes in the sun, but more frequently in the shade to avoid plants losing their color. It can also be done on mats, in barns, under temporary shelters, or in other structures created for this purpose. It is not used in large productions but can be an excellent solution for small and medium productions as it is low cost and has a low environmental impact. It suffers, however, from weather conditions. For this reason, it is practicable where the harvesting season coincides with periods characterized by a dry climate. Natural drying is the most common method globally, except in industrial systems or continental-humid climates, where you must always use a dryer.

Artificial drying is more efficient and essential for big productions. It is carried out in dryers, stoves, or air-conditioned rooms equipped with an artificial heat source. Large quantities of material can be dried within 48-60 hours, using low temperatures, no higher than 120°F. However, it is energy-intensive and expensive. The water is dried with a stream of dry air, passed through the material to be dried spread over large areas, even on multiple levels or trays. In the simplest artificial drying system, the air containing the moisture removed from the plant material is dispersed into the atmosphere, whereas, in the most modern system, the air is recycled to saturation thanks to process control systems. Once dried, bunches of lavender are beaten to obtain the detachment of the flowers that must be kept in glass or ceramic containers, protected from light. Lavender is easy to dry and preserve to be reused in aromatic bags or for a bouquet of dried flowers. To dry lavender, you must pick the flowers at the right time, when their color is the brightest and they smell the strongest. Depending on its end use, you can choose between drying them in a dark or sunny room. Once a sufficient amount of lavender has been gathered, you can make a bunch by taking it from the well-aligned stems. Next, it is necessary to twist a ribbon or elastic band around the base that will tighten the lavender without crushing the stems. Slowly drying lavender in a dark place helps it preserve its color. To do so, simply hang the obtained bunches in a garage, shed, or under a tree. Know that the time needed for drying also depends on the climate as a more humid area will extend the process.

COMMINUTION AND PULVERIZATION

Once dried, lavender flowers can be subjected to various processes depending on their purposes, from cosmetics to home care or aromatherapy. These operations can be carried out by herbalist companies, but also, more and more often, by farmers themselves to increase the 0-mile effect. Suppose the farm is equipped with a processing laboratory to make lavender-based products, such as cosmetics, pharmaceuticals, foods, and supplements. In that case, the starting point for packaging many of these items is the lavender chopped or pulverized as appropriate.

Similarly, even if the company is not involved in creating complex products, such as those mentioned above, you could still sell shredded and pulverized lavender to processing companies. Therefore, it is a matter of cutting, mincing, and pulverizing the dried flowers by employing special machines that process them without altering their characteristics and qualities. The machines can also detect stones, earth, dust, hair, and other materials, thus ensuring a clean, pure, and usable end product. Among other processes applicable to dry lavender flowers, comminution is the cutting or bruising of the medicinal plant using guillotine cutters, hammer mills, or fixed blade mills.

Pulverization consists of a further step of reduction of the mass constituted by the dried flowers. It allows to transform them into a very fine and impalpable powder used in subsequent processes and transformations.

DISTILLATION

Once mature, the lavender collected at the end of flowering can be distilled. Those activities that decide to invest resources, not only economically but also in terms of time and personnel, to install a distillation plant inside the buildings of the lavender garden, will be responsible for the distillation of lavender. They will be able to distill the lavender flowers and then sell the essential oil and the hydrolat to other activities, or else, to make their own cosmetics, foods, and herbal products based on lavender. After evaluating both its production capacity — in terms of essential oil and hydrolat — and the resources it intends to invest, a business can choose to produce floral oil and floral water, both for its own laboratory and for retail and wholesale sales. You must also know what the actual distillation of lavender consists of, even if you do not intent on applying this practice. This process is done by simply passing water vapor through the flowers, preferably fresh, to extract the volatile aromatic compounds and extract the essential oil. Let's now proceed to the illustration of the process.

First of all, it should be pointed out that the boiling temperature of a mixture of two immiscible liquids is lower than the boiling point of the most volatile components. For this reason, adding water, and consequently, introduce hot steam into the distillation column lowers the boiling point of the substances, allowing them to be separated by distillation. You should proceed as follows: after the cut in the field, fresh flowers destined for distillation are not harvested immediately but left to dry for about two or three days and, therefore, pre-cut in the sun. After that, lavender flowers are placed in the distiller, a container crossed by water vapor. The distiller's extraction system consists of:

- a heat source that generates steam,
- a still,
- a condenser,
- and a vase.

The steam, through the still, passes through the plant material, breaking down the tissues and carrying the odorous substances upward. The lavender is distilled at about 140-150°F — the right temperature to keep all the essential oil properties intact. The resulting mixture of water vapor and essence rises in the neck of the distiller, and then cools down in the grate, thus settling in a vase called "florentine" or "essencier." The latter is provided with two taps: the higher one is used to collect the essential oil, while the distilled water, also called hydrolat or floral water, flows in the lower one. The hydrolat is obtained by condensing steam, which brings the essential oil with it in the cooling coil. The hydrolat remains impregnated by it, although it separates from the essential oil because of their different specific weight as the essence is lighter than water. During distillation, you may use rainwater to maintain the high quality of the essential oil and floral water. After distillation, lavender plants can be used as fuel to produce steam for future distillations, or as mulch to protect soils from excessive cold and to promote biomass. Essential oil and hydrolat, instead, must undergo some treatments to prolong their duration. First of all, they must be filtered to eliminate possible impurities, pectins, mucilage, waxes, and turbidity. Then, they can be proceeded with rectification, or deterpenation, a further distillation that eliminates the terpenic fraction heavier and less odorous hydrocarbons from oil and hydrolat, and is done to improve its organoleptic characteristics. Finally, the product must be left to rest for a certain time to allow it to mature properly and season.

CONSERVATION AND PACKAGING

The distillation and creation of hydrolat or essential oil are not the only options to make with lavender, but certainly the most common ones. While waiting to be packaged, dried lavender bunches can be kept in dark and dry rooms, inside unique baskets or boxes, preferably new, clean, and dry. If you choose to reuse packaging, it must be adequately cleaned to avoid contamination with foreign bodies. These may derive from the earth and include stones, organic and inorganic fragments, residues of packaging and tools, or be dust, insects, poisonous plants or pests that may compromise the quality of the product. A preliminary check should be followed by periodic ones to ensure the warehouse is free from insect pests, such as the borer, whose larvae feed on stored plant matter, and that the containers in which the product is stored are in good condition. The humidity and ideal temperature for storage vary based on the type of product. For instance, fresh products, such as potted plants and cuttings, must be stored around 33 to 41°F. Meanwhile, dried and packaged ones must be stored in a dry and clean room, at no higher than 50°F, and with relative humidity no higher than 40%. Finally, essential oils must be stored away from light, in rooms with a constant temperature no lower than 32°F nor higher than 95°F. Concerning the packaging, to maintain the high quality of the product, it is preferable to package the lavender bunches, but also cuttings and dried flowers, in a short time to ensure that no external agent will alter the properties. As bunches and dried flowers can be sold at retail but also destined to other activities, such as organic product stores, pharmacies, and herbalist shops, which will reuse them, they can be packaged using different techniques and packaging. For the packaging of dried products for retail sale, rustic sheets of straw paper, recycled plastic bags, or decorated boxes may be used for bouquets, while glass or porcelain jars with corks can be used for flowers. All packaging intended for sale to the final consumer must indicate, on the back or bottom, the date of packaging and the product's expiration date, and emphasize their organic origin. In principle, bouquets and dried flowers destined for other activities require a less accurate aesthetic impact. Therefore, you may use cardboard or polystyrene boxes and plastic bags. In fact, the manufacturer can agree individually with the customers on the most suitable packaging, ensuring that the product is always stored optimally. The packaging of bunches and dried flowers is generally done manually by a dedicated worker or the person in charge of harvesting and drying, depending on the amount of work and the size of the business. Similarly, you can assign bottles and vials in more refined glass for retail sales, even for essential oil and floral water packaging, and in larger packages, perhaps made of plastic or tin, for wholesale. Essential oils must be stored in hermetically sealed bottles or dark glass vials because air, humidity, and light can degrade them.

Finally, even fresh products, such as plants and cuttings, may be packaged differently depending on whether they are intended for retail or wholesale. In any case, the preservation of the packaged product requires cool and dry rooms. For this reason, packaged products that are not displayed in the sales area may be stored in the same room as freshly harvested lavender.

CHAPTER 4.
EQUIPMENT

Before describing the equipment needed for a lavender garden, we must state that those who already own a farm and choose to grow lavender as an extension of their activity and a supplement to their income will already have many of the equipment listed below. Only those starting a business from scratch will need to purchase all the necessary machinery and tools, which in some cases, will not all be essential. Again, it depends on the use and investment you are willing to put in. In addition, you should consider buying used equipment considering some tools are pretty expensive. By doing so, you could lower the investment to better recoup costs later on. Also, the equipment might vary depending on the area in which you plan to undertake the laundry and the type of finished products you decide to offer. For example, if you choose to start medium-to-large-sized cultivation, you will have to equip yourself with a more performing tractor and devices for the automation of sowing. Instead, for a small-scale activity, harvesting, drying, and other processes can be done manually using small and simple tools. Nothing is impossible, even though at first, the amount of equipment needed may seem expensive. There are many ways to make up for this equipment, and in some cases, it is even possible to rent or hire the main mechanical cultivation equipment. This chapter will look in detail at the equipment needed to start and maintain profitable lavender cultivation.

AGRICULTURAL EQUIPMENT FOR CULTIVATION

- Motor cultivator
- Tractor
- Trailer
- Tiller or spading machine
- Seeder
- Transplanter

- Pump sprayer
- Harvesting machine (reaper)
- Mulching cloth
- Forks, rakes, awls, and other minute soil cultivation tools
- Potting tools

LABORATORY AND OTHER ROOM FURNISHINGS AND EQUIPMENT

The need for tools necessary for the phase following the actual cultivation, namely, the realization of products intended for trade, and therefore, remunerative, should not be underestimated.

- Cutting machine for shredding
- Distillation equipment
- Dryer
- Lighting system
- Minute tools for processing lavender
- Warehouse furniture
- Work and drying tables
- Signs
- Packaging and wrapping
- Sales area furniture
- Vehicle

OFFICE FURNITURE AND EQUIPMENT

A company that wants to call itself wholly professional and that leaves nothing to chance should never underestimate the need to develop a strategic plan, which also includes an office and its furniture and essential tools, including:

- Computers
- Landline phones and voicemail
- Smartphones
- Software
- Printers
- And other computer equipment.

AGRICULTURAL EQUIPMENT FOR CULTIVATION

So, let's see specifically the main equipment provided to those who want to start cultivating lavender, from the first phase to the sale. All these tools are to be considered when drawing up your start-up's business plan, in some cases, to obtain specific subsidies provided by some countries that encourage the healthy and beneficial use of land.

- **TRACTOR**. This machinery is useful for preparing the land on which to plant the lavender cultivation, post-harvest work, and fertilizing. The most modern wheeled tractors and, above all, tracked tractors, can move skillfully in small spaces and adapt to uneven terrains, as impervious as those on which one decides to undertake the cultivation of lavender may be. The cutting-edge ergonomics of some tractors allow for a driving style not far removed from that of a good off-road car, with an adjustable seat, telescopic steering wheel, hydrostatic steering, and integral platform. Tractors come equipped with modern safety features, optional air conditioning, and can shoot with confident balances, even in the tightest spaces. Many models can be fitted with the main working tools, namely tillers, spades, and pruning shears. There also are practical isodiametric tractors on the market, characterized by four wheels of the same diameter. This aspect means that these tractors, lower and narrower than traditional ones, have a tiny footprint, which allows them to agilely pass everywhere, even in the narrowest and steepest passages.

- **MOTOR CULTIVATOR**. The motor-cultivator is a valid alternative to the tractor. It is generally used for experimental crops and on small scale, which does not make it convenient or appropriate to operate with a large machine and high costs and consumption. Modern motor cultivators have evolved into an increasingly complete and versatile range. They are available with various powers, from 5 to 20 horsepower. Many are multi-purpose and stand out for their safety of use. They can be equipped with a wide range of work equipment, from an adjustable tiller to a plow, from a mower to a spade and sprayer units, to mechanize crop operations as much as possible. They are indispensable for those who intend to carry out their activity professionally, while those who choose to start gradually — and cultivate lavender on a small plot or in a greenhouse — can do without them.

- **TRAILER**. A trailer can be useful for transporting the bunches of lavender collected in baskets, as well as equipment, plows, spades, shovels, etc., while working the land. There is a wide range of farm trailers of various sizes depending on your needs and the size of your operation.

- **TILLER OR SPADE.** A rotary tiller is used to break up clods of soil when preparing the ground for planting and cleaning the soil. The working part of this tool consists of a horizontal-axis rotor connected to the hoes that work the soil. The hoes can have different shapes, depending on the soil to be worked. As an alternative to the tiller, you may use a spading machine, an agricultural machine designed for tilling the soil. It works like a manual spade, as it completely overturns the clod of soil. Spades' numbers are generally variable, from 4 to 32, and carried by arms that pivot at the upper end of the cranks of a crankshaft. The machine can work at a depth ranging from 4 to 23 inches. It is carried to the rear or front by the walking tractor or tractor and receives motion from the power take-off. The shaft's speed varies through a gearbox. A hood with touching strips or struts can be applied to the rear of the spading machine for soil finishing. Some spading machines are equipped with a rear power take-off arranged for connection to another machine to allow combined working.

- **SEEDER**. This is a valuable piece of equipment in extensive cultivations to plant lavender seeds in previously prepared soil. The seeder, towed by the tractor, can make, in a single pass, the seeding furrow, the deposition of seeds, and clods' recompacting above the furrow. Nowadays, the most widely used seed drills are precision seed drills, which are capable of achieving any distance in the seed placement. These are equipped with a pneumatic device operated by the tractor that constantly produces a depression. You can collect the single seed in the hopper employing rotating metal distributors equipped with tiny holes. The depression is applied to one side of the surface, so that only one seed per hole is sucked in from the other side, by depression. When the vacuum is released, the seeds fall into the distributors to be sown. The mechanical movement of the distributors, whose speed determines the spacing, is carried out by wheels resting on the ground. In this way, we obtain a constant spacing, even when the driving speed varies.

- **TRANSPLANTER**. Although we can manually plant lavender and lavandin cuttings, in extensive cultivations, it is advisable to use a semi-automatic transplanter, which can help the operator transplant the cuttings into the ground precisely and quickly. The automatic transplanter, on the other hand, is hooked to the walking tractor or tractor and is equipped with a distributor with rotating perforating cups (from 1 to 6) and a change of ratios that allow an adjustment of the distance on the row from 7 ¾ to almost 78 ¾ inches. It can also be equipped with row markers and fertilizer spreaders.

- **PUMP SPRAYER.** Since fungi can affect the yield of the lavender field, it may be useful to have pest control equipment deal with unexpected cryptogamic diseases and other emergencies. The simplest and most economical method is to acquire a sprayer pump, a piece of equipment used to apply insecticides, fungicides, and disinfectants through a lance with adjustable sprayers. The easiest to use and smallest models of sprayers are knapsack sprayers, while more sophisticated models can be mounted on any tractor model.

- **HARVESTING MACHINE.** To harvest lavender inflorescences in medium/large crops, it is possible to use a reaper-binder, a mounted, towed, or self-propelled machine that cuts and binds the product in small sheaves. Such model can come in the form of a machine equipped with a practical gearbox with four forward gears and a reverse one, driven by a single-cylinder diesel engine, equipped with a differential with locking and brakes with independent controls on the two wheels, which allow to maneuver the machine optimally on any terrain. The harvester is available in two versions: a simple one, for plants whose height does not exceed 27 ½ - 31 ½ inches from the ground, and one with a raised frame, to make the plants whose height exceeds 31 ½ inches from the ground flow under the bridge. The cutting width is on average 4 ½ feet, and the cutter bar is available with regular teeth or anti-clogging teeth. Thanks to their continuous and constant movement, the forks positioned above the cutter bar allow conveying the cut product toward the tying device. Finally, the knotter regulates the binding of the cut crop and the cutting of the twine once the sheaf has been prepared, the diameter of which can be adjusted in various sizes using a special spring. They are generally small machines, which, due to their low cost and practicality, are like the old grain reaper-binders used on hilly terrains.

- **MULCHING SHEET.** A polypropylene mulching sheet can be laid on the soil to protect and preserve it from weeds. Polypropylene is a fabric that prevents the passage of light, inhibiting the growth of weeds around crops and walkways. It also allows the soil to absorb rainwater or water from irrigation. Finally, it also facilitates the installation of pots and agricultural structures. As far as smaller crops are concerned, the cover can be replaced by ingredients of natural origin, such as barks or straws, or, as seen above, residues of the distillation practice.

- **FORKS, RAKES, AWLS, AND OTHER MINUTE TOOLS FOR CULTIVATING THE SOIL.** You will need various tools to facilitate manual agricultural work. The main ones include forks, rakes, hoes, tillers, transplanting awls, shovels, areolas, wide brooms, and wide and narrow transplanters. The range of working tools is enriched and improved every day to facilitate and make the various phases of cultivation and the different cultural operations more effective.

- **TOOLS FOR GROWING IN POTS.** To efficiently carry out all the operations required for growing lavender in pots, tools such as hoes, small transplanters, shovels, and rakes will be helpful. These tools simulate the large equipment used for working the soil. Still, they are small and can be found practically anywhere, and are not always necessary, although they significantly improve the resulting quality of work. These tools can be purchased individually or together in so-called "gardening kits," and are usually made of metal with plastic or wooden handles.

FURNITURE AND EQUIPMENT LABORATORY AND OTHER PREMISES

Here, we see, in a few words, all that is necessary to set up the rooms where the phases of processing, storage, and sale of lavender and other products take place. First, you must have signs and placards. If you have a company store, the choice of the sign is crucial as it allows potential customers to identify and recognize the activity from a distance and conveys a first general impression of the activity. Therefore, the image chosen for the sign must reflect, through a pleasant and recognizable logo, the particularity of the activity and its characteristics. There are different types of signs, with different shapes and colors. Still, given the activity's agricultural nature, you could focus on rustic decorations or a sign made of wood or wrought iron handmade, which recalls, through shapes and colors, the typical aroma of lavender. It may only be worthwhile to choose a bright sign if the farm is located on the roadside or visible from the cars driving on the highway or provincial roads. If you are directly selling at your farm, and thus, presumably in a non-urban area, you can also install a series of signs leading to the access road. These will make your business more visible and allow customers to reach it more easily.

For the rooms where the sorting, hulling, processing, and packaging of the product take place, LED spotlights or ceiling lights can ensure excellent visibility to the operators. The lighting system is indeed essential in such cases, as it can make the environment more pleasant and functional in the sales area. Therefore, you must set up a system that offers good and healthy visibility while avoiding shadows or blinding lights and highlighting the assortment of products on sale. Stores often resort to intense and bright lighting made of neon or metal halide lights that guarantee a good color rendering. These can be recessed "director" or placed inside chandeliers or, in some cases, inside the display structures. For more significant energy savings, you could even resort to LED lighting in this room or install solar panels that will allow you to take advantage of an independent and natural source of energy against a small initial investment. Calculating the consumption required by the cultivation of a given product is often very relevant for the final buyer of that product as they will know they have bought an organic and natural product that has not damaged the planet in any way.

LED spotlights or ceiling lights are indispensable for hulling and sorting the bunches and flowers of lavender on the worktables, which will also be used to package the finished products. Depending on the layout of the premises where the processing takes place, you may purchase two or more worktables. To carry out manual operations with optimal hygiene, you can buy a stainless-steel table. The surface must be smooth, without grooves that could channel annoying residues of raw material, wide and, possibly, wheeled, to facilitate the movement.

The **DRYER** represents an essential place for the activity. Besides being exposed to direct sunlight or being placed in a greenhouse, lavender bunches can be dried utilizing a dryer with term ventilation, thus eliminating the free water present in the plant. Dryers with term ventilation provide heat and ventilation in the plants' environment. You may dry in a dehumidified air cell at low temperature by lowering the air humidity through special suction equipment. The dehumidification occurs through an energetic cooling with the re-introduction in circulation of the air itself, after having brought it to the preset temperature. This procedure allows the creation of a continuous circle of increasingly dry air, which causes the elimination of water through evaporation. The evaporated water, transferred to the plant, is condensed and drained.

The **CUTTER** is the machine that provides for the cutting of the plant before or after drying to produce dried medicinal herbs in different cuts, among which is herbal tea. A small instrument that offers great advantages and possibilities, the cutter represents a reasonable initial investment. Electrically powered, it is equipped with inlet and outlet rollers of the material "trimmed" by special cutting tools contained in the central body of the machine.

Modern electric cutters are equipped with a cutting system capable of reproducing the manual operation to keep the product very compact. Those machines are made of stainless steel and feature self-sharpening blades and easily removable parts to guarantee a complete and quick cleaning.

The most used distillers by farms are **STEAM DISTILLERS**. The structure of a distillation plant consists of a burner, combined with a boiler used to generate steam; a still that comes in various sizes and consists of the boiler, loading chamber, and grate; a capital with a distillation column that allows the mixture to condense; a serpentine cooler, and a decanter, Florentine vase, or "essencier." Almost all currently used distillers are of discontinuous load ones, that is with interruption of distillation for the loading and unloading of the drug.

We may use small tools for the pruning of lavender and lavandin, such as knives with a well-sharpened blade, cutters, or strong and sharp scissors. Knives and scissors, which must always be cleaned before use to avoid infecting the plant, must be well handy to carry out the operations efficiently. Instead, manual or electric cutters and grinders should be used for comminuting and pulverizing dried flowers. Also, do not forget that you will need packaging and packing. As previously mentioned, fresh and dried products deriving from cultivation will be packaged differently according to whether they are fresh or dried and to their selling destination (retail or wholesale). Below, we briefly describe the main types of packaging and wrapping used for various products.

● **BASKETS**. Baskets are first used to transport the bunches harvested from the cultivation to the premises for sorting and hulling, and then, to transport to the drying room and/or distillation plant. Baskets of various sizes and shapes are made of wicker, rattan, rush, or pith.

- **SACKS**. Sacks may be used for storing seeds and cuttings. These can contain 11 to 33 lbs. and can either be disposable, made of plastic, or reusable materials, such as fabric or paper.

- **SACHETS AND BAGS**. To pack dried herbs and flowers, such as *potpourri*, you can use small, glossy plastic, or straw paper bags of various sizes. The producer can ask the reference printing house to print, on the back of the packaging, the custom realization of the sachets, along with the list of the main beneficial characteristics of lavender, to inform and advise the consumer.

- **JARS, BOTTLES, AND VIALS**. Lavender essential oil and flower essence can be bottled and sold in glass jars, flasks, and vials. Glass turns out to be the ideal material for such containers as it does not yield any element to its content, no matter how long it remains in contact with it. It is easy to seal, even without professional machinery, thus ensuring a good hermeticity. Glass jars, flasks, and vials can be sealed with corks.

You must consider a series of furnishings provided for the different areas of the business. Today, with the possibility of reaching everywhere thanks to the internet, it may seem obsolete. Still, the cultivation of lavender follows the rhythms and times of the earth and remains firmly anchored to it. For this reason, it is necessary to acquire furniture dedicated to the warehouse. If you have a room for storing tools, consumables, packaging, jars, bags, other containers, finished products, and more, it is practical to set it up with sturdy shelves made of metal or wood. You can also buy drawer units, cabinets, plastic boxes, containers, and everything that allows you to store your equipment.

Moreover, even with good e-commerce and excellent online and social communication, you must physically showcase the products, and therefore, have proper furniture for the sales area. To set up this area, besides the counter for the cash register, you need some shelving to display the products on sale. Depending on the type and variety of products, you can also use some wall, gondola, or table displays, as well as large baskets of straw or wicker to place the fragrant bouquets of lavender. Depending on the image and style you want to give to the sales area, the furniture can be made of different materials. Given the nature of the lavender garden, wood or wrought iron would be preferable. Living in the countryside and reaching stores or warehouses, you must foresee the frequent use of a car. A means of transport can certainly be useful if you must deliver products to stores, markets, or final customers. Given the type of products, you may not necessarily need a large vehicle. You can use an open box van or a tarpaulin, for instance, with the possibility of uncovering and covering the vehicle. To limit the investment, you may buy a used vehicle.

BUILDINGS

Whoever chooses to start a lavender farm must consider the possibility of setting up one or more buildings for the processing, storage, and sale of the finished product. If you already own a farm and have an unused masonry structure, you can divide it into the necessary rooms. Alternatively, it is possible to buy some prefabs, container or wooden types, or simple boxes of a few square meters to be placed inside or near the crops. Besides, the structural characteristics of buildings and equipment are regulated by specific regional and/or municipal regulations. Whoever chooses to start this activity must have a thorough knowledge of the legislation in their area and ask for prior opinions from the local health authorities of reference. Given the complexity of the topic, you may want to seek the advice of a professional technician who has already worked in the same municipality.

The size of buildings should vary according to the products and services offered. Generally, based on the format chosen, the following spaces should be present in the building:

AN AREA FOR SORTING AND HULLING. This area does not need to be vast, nor specifically equipped. Having clean tables (usually in stainless steel) is enough to arrange the freshly picked lavender. It is not advisable, however, to wash the lavender — the water remaining in the bunches would lengthen the time needed for their drying, making the process more onerous and expensive, and would favor dangerous fermentation processes. Therefore, you do not need to equip the room with washing tubs. As sorting and peeling require a lot of attention, it will be imperative for the room to be well lit, for example, with spotlights or LED lights, to provide workers with the best working conditions. This room should be well-ventilated and not humid.

A DISTILLATION AREA. This is the area where the distillation plant will be located. Of course, its size will vary according to the size of the distillation plant, which will depend, in turn, on the production volume of the lavender farm. The distillation room should also be dry and well-ventilated and have an adequate lighting system and easily sanitized floors and walls, possibly tiled or PVC.

A DRYING AREA. If it does not naturally occur in the open air, the drying process of lavender may be undertaken in a greenhouse, within which the temperature will have to constantly remain around 95/105°F. These temperatures ensure optimal hygienic conditions, safeguarding the active principles, and the organoleptic qualities of the products. But, as we have previously seen, you can also dry lavender in a — dark, dry, warm, and well-ventilated — closed room where the oven or the dryer with thermo-ventilation will be placed. Inside this room, you can reduce light to a minimum and install shading nets and fans near the doors to facilitate air exchange.

A PROCESSING AND PACKAGING WORKSHOP. This may coincide with the room destined for sorting and trimming. The laboratory must be large enough to contain the tools necessary for these operations, any other process related to the lavender cultivation, and parts of the packaging. To optimize processing, this area should be well lit. To get functional lighting and save energy, you may install LED spotlights or ceiling lights. However, to best preserve the raw materials being processed, the workshop should also be easy to darken. Curtains or blinds can be placed over the openings for this purpose. Since the basic characteristics of the workshop must be hygiene and functionality, the flooring must be made of easily washable and non-slip material, such as rubber, PVC, or linoleum. You can also cover or tile the walls to make them easily sanitized. You must also have multi-functional workbenches, adaptable to different production operations, as well as furniture, drawer units, trolleys, shelves, and racks to hold raw materials and position and store equipment.

A WAREHOUSE FOR MACHINES, TOOLS, AND CONSUMABLES. This will be useful to store machinery, agricultural implements, and tools necessary to maintain agricultural machinery, seeds, cuttings, fertilizers, and pesticides. The optimal size of the warehouse depends on the number and type of machines and tools you have. Either way, this space must be utilized to its fullest, with efficient use of space and functional shelving and racks. To store plant protection products, pesticides, and other similar agricultural products, you must use a safety cabinet that complies with current regulations and has standard signage on the doors.

A WAREHOUSE FOR STORAGE OF FINISHED PRODUCTS AND PACKAGING. The workshop area can be used as a warehouse for storing dried lavender and other products awaiting packaging. This room should be cool and dry and can also be used for storing pallets of jars, boxes, vials, caps, cardboard bags, and various containers needed for packaging the lavender, as well as boxes for shipping or delivering goods, etc. Having a room to store these supplies allows you to buy them in large quantities from wholesalers to benefit from significant savings in money and time as you reduce the number of orders. In any case, this space must be used to its fullest, with efficient use of space and functional furniture.

A SALES AREA AT THE GROW HOUSE. For the direct sale of lavender and lavender products, you may set up a sales area near the cultivation. This can occupy part of the surface of the covered premises and should be tastefully and simply furnished. In case of direct selling, it is indispensable to place, in this area, a counter equipped with a cash register and some shelves where lavender plants, dried bunches, essential oil, and other lavender products can be displayed. Even if it is not a real store, the products should be made visible so that customers can see them, possibly even without the help of staff. This can be done by placing one or more displays. According to studies, on the way from the entrance to the checkout, the items that attract the most attention are those on the right-hand side. Therefore, it is preferable to dedicate this area to the display of the products considered more attractive to clients and more profitable for the firm. The same applies to the space between 2 ½ feet and 5'3 above the floor, in which customers will be most interested, and to the so-called "meditation zone," which refers to the checkout counter, where customers waiting to be served or to pay are most likely to make impulse purchases.

OFFICE AND TOILETS. Such an area can be used to set up a small office to deal with relationships with suppliers and clients and, in general, with management. One or more desks, a few ergonomic chairs, some shelving, and a few cabinets are enough. The office should be equipped with a landline telephone, a business cellphone, an answering machine, a fax machine, a computer, and a printer. This area can also be used for staff toilets, which must comply with the Local Health Authority's regulations. They must therefore be equipped with an anti-bathroom and well ventilated.

CHAPTER 5.
TEAM WORK

The staff needed to run a lavender farm varies according to the size and organization of the business, the range of services and products offered, and the division of labor. In most cases, cultivation is started gradually, perhaps starting with family-run cultivation operations. As a result, production is initially limited and management thoroughly carried out by the owner, who may also take care of the cultivation, processing, and sales of the products. But, one person usually cannot know how to do everything and how to oversee many things at the same time. Often, those who undertake lavender cultivation are the owners of a farm, who, therefore, can count on staff who is already qualified and able to carry out various tasks. Having a team of dedicated professionals to rely on is essential for anyone who wants to set out on this adventure on their own. In addition to permanent workers, some occasional workers may be needed to help the owner during the harvesting phase, and in general, when most of the work is concentrated. If it works, over time, the activity can grow by enriching the quantities and types of products offered and by offering various services, such as organizing visits of the lavender grove, workshops, and training courses, thus increasing the staff. In the cultivation of large areas, the help of family assistants, occasional or seasonal collaborators, or permanent employees will become essential, especially for the harvesting and drying operations.

Also, very much in vogue in recent years, is the possibility of receiving help from young people, including foreigners, in exchange for room and board. With the help of specific portals that put volunteers in contact with agricultural activities worldwide, these young people are willing to cross oceans and continents to live and take on rural activities for a few weeks or months. It is true that having a team of people you can count on, including remote workers who handle online sales, the website, and order sorting, means making a quantum leap and pushing your business to maximum efficiency. In this way, the number of tasks that need to be organized in the best possible way and distributed throughout the year, based on the number of staff available, can be numerous.

LAVENDER CULTIVATION

Since this is an agricultural activity, the owner is responsible for the technical tasks related to the cultivation of lavender. They must have the necessary skills to work and prepare the soil, must know the botanical characteristics and needs of the species of lavender cultivated, its vegetative cycle, the techniques of sowing, planting, and transplanting, and the most appropriate fertilization and weeding practices. It is possible to specialize in lavender cultivation by following training courses organized by consortia and trade associations, inquiring with other potential growers in the area or taking an online video course. These sources will be helpful to learn about the appropriate cultivation methods depending on the type of soil and the climate in the area where one wants to start the activity, as well as the traditional working techniques and the most suitable periods for sowing, planting, and harvesting. During the seeding/planting and harvesting phases, when more intensive labor is needed, the owner can be helped by one or more collaborators — usually family members in the case of a family business. In addition to the necessary technical skills, the entrepreneurial role played by the owner is also fundamental and becomes increasingly important as the land cultivated and the volume of business increases. The following tasks are not strictly "technical" but are fundamental for the management and success of the activity. First is the promotion of the lavender farm on the local market through the most effective actions to find new customers and retain those acquired. Then, they need to know how to manage the relationship with suppliers; deal with hygiene and safety standards, and in general bureaucracy; decide what products and services to offer; control the general trend of the activity; keep the company's accounts; maintain contact with banks, accountants, and trade associations; and coordinate the work of employees. To carry out these tasks properly, one must have a natural predisposition to interpersonal relationships and direct contact with customers to satisfy the organized workshops' participants and those who will come to visit the company. Of course, one person does not necessarily possess all these skills.

Thus, many of these tasks must be divided among close and specialized collaborators.

HARVESTING, SORTING, AND HULLING

These operations usually require most of the time dedicated to lavender cultivation. They should be performed by skilled hands, capable of not compromising the quality of the final product with trivial mistakes. However, these tasks can also be fulfilled by the owner who, if necessary, can delegate to one or more assistants, especially in medium or large cultivations. If the owner needs to use external, inexperienced personnel, they should give them instructions to obtain accurate work as well as supervise the entire process.

DRYING, DISTILLATION, AND PACKAGING

Depending on the amount of raw material collected, these tasks can be carried out by one or more people, who will then carry out the normal drying, distillation, and packaging stages. Employees will also help keep the laboratory, equipment, sorting, and worktable clean. The number of required employees depends primarily on the quantities produced. Technical knowledge acquired through experience is also essential for processing and packaging.

SALES

Whether selling to stores, pharmacies, herbalists, and processors, the owner will agree directly with the managers on these activities and define the mode of delivery, price, and packaging upstream to recoup the production costs. It will be possible to organize a system of withdrawal of the raw material in the company or, eventually, to offer home delivery if one is equipped with specific cars. Instead, the direct sale in the company will be a necessary task in the case in which, in addition to plants, bunches, cuttings, and dried flowers, other products derived from them are sold, such as food, cosmetics, or products for household cleaning. Therefore, there is an offer such as to justify a sales area. In this regard, one may choose whether to open the store only when customers arrive, making sure that they are notified by a bell/intercom/phone, to sell at set times and days, or to serve the customer at longer hours or at any time of the day. The person in charge of the sale is also responsible for stocking the shelves where the products are displayed, keeping the premises tidy, and maintaining a well-stocked warehouse. No specific skills are required for this, apart from knowledge of the products and the necessary courtesy and availability to work with the public.

EDUCATIONAL ACTIVITY

Once the cultivation has been expanded and the number of activities has increased, you may offer didactic courses for schools and families to let them know about your activity and the techniques of cultivation and processing of the lavender plant. This role can often be filled by external professionals or by one of the members of the family or team — maybe someone who has followed the professional courses provided by the region in which the farm is located. The didactic animators are in charge of following the guests throughout the visit, and their number must be adequate to the number of people participating in the visits. In school groups, the operator will also have to plan the educational activities together with the teachers. To carry out this role, one must be able to valorize local productions, have knowledge of pedagogy and management of interpersonal relations, and know the basics of territorial marketing. Finally, it is a good idea to let the owner take care of the training courses and consultancy for those who want to learn how to cultivate lavender and lavandin professionally, as they will have a lot to teach given the experience, and perhaps, the certification they acquired throughout the process.

CHAPTER 6.
PEST CONTROL AND PREVENTION

Pest control is necessary even though lavender is a plant particularly resistant to the attacks of animals, parasites, and fungi. Indeed, some pathogens, such as Armillaria Mellea, Rosellinia Necatrix, and Coniothyrium lavandulae, can cause root or collar rot, whereas others, such as Phoma and Septoria lavandulae, are responsible for damages to the buds. Among insects, Diptera, Thomasiniana and Resseliella lavandulae, the beetle Arima marginata, and some Lepidoptera, such as Heliothis peltigera and Alucita tetradactyla, can harm the aerial part of the lavender and Lavandula, whereas Ephestia elutella can deteriorate the stored product.

One of the most annoying and challenging problems for plants is thrips, which mainly occur in indoor growing. Like many other types of pests, thrips attach themselves to the structure of the plant and can be seen on the leaves and suck the sap. These small insects represent one of the biggest problems for all growers, especially those who deal with greenhouse and indoor cultivations, in part because they reproduce up to 12 times a year. When they reach adulthood, they start flying from one plant to another. They are about 1.5 mm (0,59 inches) long and are visible to the naked eye, deposited in the upper part of the leaves, which are cut and covered with white spots while the small black spots that you may find are nothing more than their excrements. To prevent the spreading of this species, you must keep the environment clean and disinfected. Garlic or neem oil, for example, are effective allies against thrips infestation.

Aphids are known as plant lice, are black and small, feed on nymphs, and mainly nest on leaves. They are very annoying for the vegetable garden because they often transmit viruses to plants, damaging some vegetables. After sucking sap, they crumple leaves, thus affecting the most tender parts of the plant. To get rid of aphids, check crops very often and remove them at the first infestation, for example, by pruning affected branches or using water jets. Neem oil is again an effective remedy, and pyrethrum, a natural insecticide which, although toxic and harmful for good insects, such as bees, is allowed as a natural remedy.

Aleurodes, better known as whiteflies, are widespread in tropical regions and their damage can result in the loss of entire crops. Some of these species have become cosmopolitan and have reached more temperate areas. They attack both herbaceous and woody plants belonging to the Angiosperms. In greenhouses, we use biological control, which exploits the antagonistic relationships between living beings, to combat the parasitic infestation of whiteflies.

To avoid the attack of these parasites, at the beginning of spring, in concomitance with the rising of the temperatures, it is good to apply a preventive treatment, preferably with an organic insecticide, to the soil when there are no flowers yet. The biological insecticides allowed by the regulation are azadirachtin and spinosad. Azadirachtin has very low toxicity. For this reason, its compound is harmless for humans and vertebrates. Its environmental impact is also very low; it shows a remarkable selectivity toward useful entomofauna, including bees, so it is also compatible with biological control. It degrades in the soil in a few days. It is an insecticide of vegetable origin, extracted from the neem tree, which must be used at the first signs of infestation. It is found commercially under the trade name Azactiva or Neemazal-T/S. Like azadirachtin, spinosad is also a widely used insecticide in organic practice, although up to 15 days must elapse between the last treatment and harvesting.

Finally, to fight snails, it is possible to use proper biological snailsicide or, more simply, to sprinkle the plant's collar with ash or sand to create a physical barrier against these animals. In this case, too, you must act promptly. Slugs stay away from sand, salt, sawdust, ashes, and coffee grounds because these substances tend to dehydrate their body, which is made of 90% of water. Another method, perhaps rather cruel, is to sprinkle the ground with crushed eggshells. These being sharp, they will bother the snail's tiny body as it crawls. To keep them away, remember that snails hate copper so that you can place wires of this metal around your cultures. Also, snails detest some scents produced by certain aromatic plants, the most notable ones being aromatic plants, such as sage, garlic, nettle, and chili pepper. Among them are also mint, rosemary, fennel, parsley, and finally, basil.

CHAPTER 7.
10 MOST COMMON MISTAKES

Now that we've laid out the main ways to start, manage, and maintain a lavender crop, let's see what the most common mistakes a novice grower can make are.

CHOOSE SOIL WITH WATERLOGGING. Pre-checking the soil is essential before starting to grow lavender, essentially because soil with poor drainage is not suitable for lavender, which grows in rather dry, clayey, well-drained soil. Controlling the pH of the soil is another fundamental variation when it comes to this type of cultivation. Moreover, as we have previously seen, the soil must be previously prepared and well-oxygenated to allow all essential components to grow into healthy and robust plants.

DISREGARD SUN EXPOSURE. Lavender is a perennial plant whose highest peculiarity is its flowers, scent, color, beauty, and the products that can be obtained from them, such as the precious officinal oil. A flourishing lavender is a lavender that receives proper care. For example, it is pruned when necessary and planted in a very sunny spot, it will produce more flowers, and therefore, more essential oil and derived products. And as a result, revenues will be higher.

DO NOT CALCULATE THE SPACE BETWEEN ROWS NEEDED TO GROW THE LAVENDER BUSH. Keeping the lavender spaced out allows you to go between plants with the proper medium to remove weeds.

DO NOT REMOVE WEEDS, ESPECIALLY IF THE SEEDLINGS ARE TINY AND BEING SMOTHERED. For this reason, mulching may be the most economical and proactive solution.

DISREGARD THE SCENIC EFFECT. The lavender field is a beautiful, aesthetically appealing crop. The field itself represents an interesting source of income, exploitable for workshops, events, photoshoots, ceremony locations, videos, and much more. Overall, the gardening landscape can gain a lot from lavender.

DO NOT CALCULATE POTENTIAL INVESTMENTS FROM THE BEGINNING OF THE ACTIVITY. Many may give up on their dream because they had not accounted for all the costs involved in running, maintaining, and promoting the business. Every company requires a good business plan, drawn up based on expected expenses, while always keeping in mind a buffer for the unforeseen ones. It is not simply a matter of considering the cost of agricultural machinery, but also those of promotion, which are fundamental for the good performance of the structure.

THINKING YOU DO NOT NEED ANYONE. Although you may initially be able to do without too many employees, a family and organic farm cannot run itself and you will inevitably need help from professionals in various fields, for example, consultants or marketing experts who can advise you on the best strategies for promoting your business online.

DO NOT FIX LAVENDER WHEN IT IS FREEZING. Although lavender is a perennial plant and some species can withstand quite low temperatures very well, you must take precautions when winter comes and the first-night frosts occur.

DISREGARD SPECIFIC LAVENDER VARIETIES. As we have seen, not all lavenders are the same, although they look alike. Each one has a particular smell, color, shape, and effect. Choosing the most profitable species for most planted specimens is undoubtedly beneficial, after which you can experiment with more lavender species.

DO NOT PROVIDE PREVENTIVE CONTROL OF PESTS IN THE AREA. Mushrooms or parasites can compromise entire cultivations. Thus, you must keep most of the parasites away, even by using ingredients of natural origin, and therefore, maintain biodiversity and respect the rules of organic cultivation.

CHAPTER 8.
SELLING LAVENDER

For a lavender farm and any other business, selling a product is not an activity that necessarily has to be complicated. It is essential not to be frightened by all the variables, but to plan and implement simple techniques to be able to bring the results home. Experience is on the side of the seller, so they must know how to exploit it. Whoever cultivates lavender learns to know it down to the smallest details to understand the products they obtain from it and be able to carry out this experience into sales. Thus, continuing to study, update, and know all the sides of a product will not only allow them to answer the possible questions of final consumers and clients, but also to carry their passion and love for the activity into the sales department. Above all, when selling, one must focus on the advantages and benefits one offers because people tend to make their purchases on an emotional level rather than pondering too much. Structuring one's sale by considering the specific benefits of a customer's needs is an effective, and above all, persuasive way to propose lavender and its side products.

To do so, you may ask yourself the following questions:

1. In what ways can the product be used to make a customer's life better?

2. How long can it be used for? Does it last a long time?

3. Is it exclusive?

4. In which position does it put the client?

In the case of a lavender field, referring to the product's authenticity and its local and environmentally sustainable production is an interesting way to approach a cross-section of customers. This is also very useful for presenting your product correctly to the proper customer segmentation. Offering a tailored product communication that is complete and provides the possible information is the only way to start selling. Therefore, you must make sure that all information is presented clearly and precisely. You will also be required to take care of the graphic and, above all, scenic presentation of the product to strike immediately and make an effective sale. Knowing the product and having previously structured efficient communication for each specific niche will allow you to act in advance and anticipate the needs of the market and end consumers.

Understanding their needs, taking them into account, and offering personalized services is the perfect way to build customer loyalty.

1. What are their motivations for buying?

2. What do they need?

3. Do you know their specific data?

Answering these questions will give you an idea of who they are and help you personalize your communication by getting in touch with their needs and knowing how your product can fulfill their aspirations or satisfy their wants.

CREATING BUYER PERSONAS

To do all that has been described so far, a business must know what the buyer personas of reference are. Let us see precisely who they are and how to identify them to take sales to the next level. Not referring to an indistinct mass but to a specific target is a marketing strategy that must be taken seriously because it is the only way to achieve acceptable results. A buyer persona is a portrait of the average user that the segment of the public you want to reach refers to — either a generalized representation, but as specific as possible, of the ideal client of a company.

The first step to create a particular target is to refer to the data. Beginning a study of the customers is the foremost way to get the information you need, and that is why budgeting the possibility of having customers fill out questionnaires, study specific interviews and insights from the site and social will allow you to build, together with the sales team, a detailed reference of what is the most suitable target for the products you intend to sell.

The information needed in creating a specific frame of reference is:

- Complete demographic data. This includes income level, age, gender, geolocation, and household.

- Occupational position. This refers to the ideal client's target occupational field and at what level they perform their work.

- Additional characteristics. Knowing their aspirations, goals, beliefs, and values is crucial to detail the target audience. For example, in this case, it could be people who want to lead a healthy life, use BIO products, and support local businesses.

All the data entered, if analyzed and crossed, can define with extreme clarity, thanks to a pinch of imagination, a buyer persona as perfectly as possible. In this way, you may operate a communication based on effective sales for each customer segment.

TWO PRACTICAL TIPS TO CONSIDER DURING DIRECT SALES

After summarizing the main steps to sell a product or service, you should know some practical skills to always have a sales style that points toward success.

Get used to breaking the ice

Some extroverted people have no problem speaking in public, while some others struggle more. Luckily, anyone can become a good salesperson with practice. To succeed, you must have all the information about the product on hand, and by studying its characteristics, you can be sure that you will be able to answer every question. If necessary, prepare and repeat several times the speech you intend to make or the salient questions you think you might be asked. Also, it might not be a bad idea to write down which moves were successful and which were not at the end of the day.

Give your client time to reflect, but close the deal

Every marketing action must be carried out with confidence. Otherwise, you will not close a deal. Therefore, decision and self-confidence are fundamental weapons. Although, you must not forget about kindness, because a satisfied customer will certainly be more likely to spend money. Leaving time for customers to reflect is always a good idea as too aggressive practices can put them on the defensive and not lead to long-term, efficient results.

HOW TO INCREASE THE AVERAGE RECEIPT

Knowing and applying the rules to increase the average receipt allows you to simply and intuitively grow the amount that each customer spends for each purchase. The following techniques can be applied both online and in a physical store:

- Build customer loyalty.

- Use impulse buying as an advantage.

- Create specific packages.

- Up-sell and cross-sell

- Create special offers.

- Know which products have the most incredible sales impact.

All these techniques allow you to increase sales, and thus, help increase the company's revenue. Let us look at each of these techniques in detail.

CUSTOMER LOYALTY

On average, regular customers spend much more than twice the usual amount in a store than a passing customer. That is why thinking of methods that help create a strong, direct relationship with customers is critical to increase the average value of a receipt. If well structured, a loyalty program can bring excellent results to a local business.

Proposing a promotion that is either exclusive and reserved for users who reach a minimum spending ceiling or progressive will lead to more purchases and a better relationship with the user.

USE THE IMPULSE TO PURCHASE AS AN ADVANTAGE

Often, those who want to buy a product do not want to wait too long, and downtime can lead the consumer to give up, and therefore, make you lose the sale. So, creating a smooth buying flow is an exciting way to increase sales by simply providing potential customers who would have given up a shortcut to solving their problems. A buying impulse is also one that leads to the last-minute purchase of something considered inexpensive and beneficial. Moving those less expensive products to the checkout counter can lead to an additional small purchase before the final receipt is typed out.

CREATE SPECIFIC PACKAGES

Creating interesting product combinations is a different way of offering a customer an optimal solution that will allow the lavender fields to increase revenue. Pushing a consumer, wholesale buyer, or company to buy two different products instead of one by combining them consistently and smartly is perceived as interesting for them. Therefore, there should be packages with related products within the physical or digital store, packages with gift ideas, and even packages with some discounts applied.

UP-SELLING AND CROSS-SELLING

These are two different, commonly used methods, which, if put into practice, can bring increase the average receipt of a laundry. Both use the buyer's interest in a product as a pivot to increase their amount of expenditure. When we talk about up-selling, we are talking about a technique designed to convince customers to buy a better, more expensive version of the product they have chosen to purchase.

In many cases, when confronted with a qualitative choice, buyers can change their minds and decide to buy a higher-priced product to get more advantages and benefits. On the other hand, cross-selling is a method that intends to add another product to the expense that the customer plans to make. Correlating products, which can maximize their effectiveness if put together or offer more solutions of use, is a winning method to lead to a greater flow of purchases.

CREATING SPECIAL OFFERS

Offers using psychological marketing increase the perceived value of a product concerning its relative scarcity. Time-based offers increase sales in a limited time range but raise the amount on the average receipt by a lot over that period. Leveraging the desire to take advantage of those specific discounts will entice users to buy, sometimes increasing sales by as much as 50%. Limited offers use the psychology of exclusive and limited access to increase sales. The desire to get the exclusivity that is proposed can push many people to purchase.

Of course, special offers must always adhere to the canons of honesty and be clear. A customer who is dissatisfied because the offer they have been awarded does not correspond to reality may ask for a refund and share bad publicity about the lavender cultivation and its products.

KNOW THE PRODUCTS WITH THE MOST SIGNIFICANT IMPACT

A company should always focus on its potential. It is the best way to increase customer spending limits. Studying sales and data related to them to find out which are the most purchased products and those most appreciated by a particular market niche will allow the company to propose them more frequently and consistently, thus increasing the success of the operation, and therefore, sales.

Offering products with a high average purchase is important for a company as it provides a solid base and allows to play it safe while increasing the visibility of a product, whose effectiveness and market appeal are already known.

BUILDING A GOOD ONLINE PRESENCE

The foundation of all sales strategies is the company's website. It allows you to reach a broad audience and meet its need for sustainability, naturalness, organic, and DIY. The website and e-commerce are the ideal places to acquire visibility. If you do not have the proper knowledge, turn to a professional in online marketing to build you one. Whatever your point may be, the company's website is the main showcase and allows it to sell and be known. It must be taken care of down to the last detail. Make sure it meets the following specific criteria:

- Easy-to-memorize domain
- Displays a responsive theme for PC, tablets, and smartphones
- Offer a great user experience
- Includes all contact and location data
- Uses the right keywords for technical SEO
- Showcases equally thorough graphics and textual aspect
- Includes call-to-actions.

Your website can be associated with a blog page, on which you can post in-depth articles and an e-commerce section to direct purchase products. Whether primary or derivative, each product must have an attractive and detailed description that entices the purchase. Shipping and packaging costs must be clear from the get-go. In fact, many people give up on their carts once they discover excessive shipping costs. So, remember that transparency always rewards.

Once you open the blog, you can ask users to subscribe to the newsletter to get a percentage discount on the first purchase. In this way, you will collect several e-mail contacts to use for special offers, e-mail marketing, invitations to events or workshops, and much more. Of course, as this part also needs to be taken care of and offer maximum transparency, it is essential to always ask for permission to send this kind of update. Consider the newsletter as a great way to get in direct contact with customers, get to know them, know what they want, and talk about you and your company directly and without any intermediary medium.

In addition, a website also provides you with passive earnings by hosting banner ads that will earn you money based on the daily traffic on your website and its visibility on the search engine. A crucial step that will help you understand if your strategy is working is to see the reports regarding site traffic. From this constant monitoring of customers' movements, you will realize what is working and what is not, what customers stop to read for longer, and where they bounced instead. Statistics are an indispensable tool for online marketers who often experiment and work based on A/B tests.

HOW TO PROMOTE ON THE TERRITORY

A farm needs to establish local relationships to enrich itself with knowledge and promote its products physically and locally. To do so, several strategies are widely used, such as the classic word of mouth. With such, if the plants, cuttings, dried bunches, and lavender products are of quality, customer satisfaction will be an excellent advertising vehicle since those who were satisfied are very likely to recommend you and your products to friends and acquaintances.

Another essential strategy is to be physically easily visible by installing signs and road signs where necessary. Since it is straightforward for the cultivation and related farm store to be in a country area, the sign can be installed at the entrance of your farm. The signs must be very visible and can be placed near the activity to "accompany" the customers interested in buying the products on site.

Making yourself known in the area is not a very difficult task. Printing flyers or brochures, as well as invitations to an inauguration party, and distribute them in the main places of the country will be enough. Another classic method is undoubtedly to participate in markets, fairs, and festivals in the country. Indeed, a farm that participates in markets, fairs, and village festivals and proposes the products of its cultivation has more chances to get known on the local market.

Being present with your own stand at such events is beneficial not only to present your activity to end consumers who want to buy lavender-based products to use for cooking, body care, or the prevention of particular ailments, but also to business owners interested in buying the raw material to be processed.

The leaflets of the lavender garden must contain some essential information, such as their contact details (address, telephone, e-mail, website, and social contacts), the list of products and services offered, prices, and any promotions, as well as a mention of the quality of the lavender produced and any organic certification. It is also advisable to complete the flyer with some photos of the cultivation and any products processed by the company.

Another way to be active protagonists of the territory is to participate and network with other consortia, local authorities, and associations that work to reevaluate the place. In this way, you can become an active part of the society in which the company has settled and a local point of reference that always guarantees high-quality products. You will be promoted in local newspapers for your work or with advertising banners and will have a name and make yourself indispensable.

RETAILING

Selling a product physically is very different from selling it online. The difference here is that the salesperson can weave a real relationship with both regulars customers and tourists. The most advantageous mode of retail is to have a sales area inside the laundry. For the owner, selling the products in a company store, directly to the final consumer, is the most profitable formula. It allows them to apply higher prices and avoid the intermediation of other commercial subjects.

Moreover, selling the products on-site allows you to contain transport costs and minimize the staff's time commitment. But, doing so will also enable customers to get to know the lavender garden as a whole and closely observe the general environment in which lavender or lavandin plants grow and develop. If you do not have a dedicated sales area on your farm, you can always set up a simple, prefabricated structure assembled by specialized companies, which will be operational right away.

Alternatively, local markets remain an exciting option for direct sales and are pretty advantageous because, apart from the cost of transport and rent, there are no particular expenses nor intermediaries needed.

CHAPTER 9.
CUSTOMER SEGMENTS

Depending on the characteristics of the lavender garden's territory and the products offered in that area, it is possible to sell to different customers and take advantage of several channels, choosing the most effective one each time. Lavender cultivation has the local market as its reference segment but determining this is not enough. Indeed, a customer segment also depends on entrepreneurial choices, the quantity of products available for sale, and the characteristics of the local market. In the end, it can be decided to refer to:

- Final consumers, for whom the lavender cultivation will carry out retail sales.

- Processing companies, who, instead, will want a product that can be purchased in bulk.

- Traders who will want processed products.

A company may decide to target one or more segments of the market and do so in a specific way, providing different strategies each time. Customer segmentation is a necessary process not only for a laundry, but for any business. It involves dividing clients into groups based on specific, common characteristics to identify effective strategies for each segment. Segmenting your possible clientele allows you to make marketing choices adapted to various audience groups.

Specifically, customer segmentation serves to:

- Develop customized marketing communication aimed at hitting specific customer targets. Building a strategy based on the interests and needs of the segment maintains effective performance.

71

- Identify the best possible product promotion.

- Probe the ground to create launching opportunities for new services or products.

- Establish long-term relationships with customers.

- Create personalized communication and specific marketing activities, enabling efficient relationship building with various segments.

- Improve customer service.

Studying the territory and identifying the various marketing niches will also allow the collateral exploitation of excess production, that is, the part of the harvest that cannot be sold on the primary market, for which it is possible to identify different destination channels, such as:

- Online sales

- Horticultural markets

- Wholesalers.

A lavender farm can sell both raw material and the final processed products and can identify the following as privileged customer segments:

- Raw material processing activities

- Herbalists and perfumeries

- Organic and fair-trade stores

- End consumers

- Distributors and wholesalers

- Fair Trade Purchasing Groups. Flower stores, nurseries, and garden centers. Consortia and producer associations.

Let us get to know in detail each customer segmentation so that we can specifically target them with the most appropriate marketing strategies.

RAW MATERIAL PROCESSING ACTIVITIES

When we refer to this niche market, the purpose of the lavender farm is to establish collaborative relationships. In this case, there are many actors to turn to, from herbalists to pharmacies, as well as perfumeries interested in having a continuous supply of high-quality raw materials at a cost that can keep up with market demand. Talking about raw material, processing activities can also refer to processing industries such as the food industry, interested in essential oil, hydrolat, and the same fresh raw material. By applying advantageous prices and a constant supplier, an activity that supplies high-quality products can stand out as a privileged interlocutor. Also, processing industries, such as the food industry, need large quantities of fresh or dried lavender, essential oil, or hydrolat. When interfacing with these realities, a lavender cultivation company needs to focus its communication on the quality of the raw materials and the tests carried out on them. Certifications are significant to produce cosmetics or food. Also, make sure to agree in advance, so that these activities mention the lavender as the point of origin of the raw material.

HERBALISTS AND PERFUMERIES

When interfacing with this specific segmentation of the clientele, it is good to keep in mind which activities are limited to the sale of ready-made and packaged products to provide different services and prices, and know which ones foresee an autonomous preparation of the products that will then be offered to the public. As a practical example, in the first case, herbalists and perfumeries will be interested in buying products such as bags of dried flowers, bottles of essential oil, or floral compositions. In contrast, in the second case, they will want to ensure the quantity of the raw materials available and the quality and certainty of a continuous supply over time. In both cases, the relationship with this type of customer is direct; creating a bond of trust is easy.

BIO AND FAIR-TRADE STORES

In general, stores that sell bio and fair-trade household products or food are looking for a local and 0-mile business, which is where lavender can come into play by offering a complete and high-quality service. By providing already packaged, local, and certified products, it will be possible to attract a segment of customers that can also be an excellent advertisement for the farm.

FINAL CONSUMERS

When we talk about final consumers, we refer to a customer segment that should not be neglected — individuals who prefer to buy directly from the producer. Naturally, a single purchase is of a smaller quantity than that of other interlocutors, but the price applied and your profit margin will be higher. The final consumers can be residents or tourists passing through if the area is a tourist destination. Usually, they can be interested in:

- Dried bunches
- Essential oil
- Fresh flowers
- Lavender foods
- Packaged products
- Potted plants

Considering the two different types of final consumers, you can work on the possibilities of loyalty, promotion, and services such as home delivery. At the same time, you must be easy to find and visible for tourists and passing customers and take care of social promotion and local positioning on the website. In both cases, end consumers appreciate the link with the territory and look for products whose origin is guaranteed and certified.

DISTRIBUTORS AND WHOLESALERS

These subjects require large quantities of products, often with specific characteristics regarding their quality and packaging. In most cases, distributors and wholesalers prefer to buy crops or surplus products directly from cooperatives or consortia of local producers. They can prove to be a beneficial customer segment to absorb that amount of surplus production.

PURCHASING GROUPS

Purchasing groups have become a market reality of the current constitution but must therefore be recognized as an interlocutor with exponential growth. Specifically, these are groups of people who organize cumulative purchases from local producers and growers, as can be a lavender farm, to obtain affordable prices on genuine products that meet certain environmental and ethical requirements. They purchase products in large quantities and redistribute them among group members. These groups prefer to buy from small local producers to reduce the pollution resulting from the transport of raw materials and to enhance the local realities of the territory in terms of the ecological quality and working conditions of the people involved. Communication that focuses on the quality of raw materials, low environmental impact, and the possibilities of encouraging a consistent relationship with the territory can be effective weapons to build a relationship with these subjects.

FLOWER STORES, NURSERIES, AND GARDEN CENTERS

Local garden centers and flower stores can represent an exciting type of clientele for your lavender farm. These businesses will be mainly interested in purchasing potted seedlings and seeds in grains of lavender and lavandin, both for cultivation and ornamental. Your farm will be able to establish profitable partnerships with garden centers and flower stores.

CONSORTIA AND PRODUCER ASSOCIATIONS

This market segment deals with collecting and marketing the productions of local farms, recognizing them fair and satisfactory profit margins. To benefit from the various services that these organizations offer, the launderer must join and respect their disciplinary code. This will provide advantages, such as constant help from the cooperative in the management and sale of their productions and the possibility of being informed promptly about new regulations in the sector. Consortia and local producers' associations can provide valuable help to developing activities. They are in charge of packaging, promoting, selling, and transporting the harvest to clients, such as wholesalers, general markets, and stores, proposing themselves on the market through strength in numbers. For a lavender growing company, it can be interesting, from a promotional point of view, to boast a distinctive, well-recognized brand in the territory, such as the one representing a large consortium.

CHAPTER 10.
BEST PRODUCTS TO SELL

Numerous products can be sold from the cultivation of lavender, both for the raw material and the derived products, regardless of the lavender species.

Below, we list and describe the main lavender-based products offered on the market. The products can either be raw materials or products created with flair and creativity.

At this point, we will limit ourselves to giving you an idea of what could be made, and, above all, what is best spent on the market. Still, much is up to the originality of each of those who decide to set up their own businesses.

1. Bouquets and packages of fresh or dried flowers

2. Floral compositions

3. Essential oil

4. Hydrolat or floral water

5. Potted plants

6. Cuttings

7. Seeds

8. Potting soils and fertilizers

9. Cultivation kits

10. Baskets and gift boxes

11. Products derived from processing.

1 - BUNCHES AND PACKAGES OF FRESH OR DRIED FLOWERS

Once harvested and selected, lavender stems can be prepared in bunches or packages, in paper or plastic, and be sold in the short term at a higher price than dried bunches because to extract the precious essential oil from flowers, they must still be fresh. Usually, lavender flowers undergo the distillation process after two or three days after being harvested. The customers interested in this kind of product mainly require processing and transformation activities to obtain the essential oil of lavender to produce derived products. Fresh lavender flower bouquets could also interest private persons, restaurants, and stores for ornamental use. Fresh flowers can be packaged in bunches wrapped in sheets of straw paper, but also be loose, directly inside the space of the farm or wholesale dedicated to the processing. If you choose to sell fresh bunches online, you must carefully pack and ship the flowers picked at dawn the same morning. It is useful, in this regard, to use a fast-shipping method and ensure that the product reaches the recipient in the shortest possible time. Unlike fresh flowers, dried flowers are not used for the distillation and extraction of essential oil. However, in addition to being of interest to individuals in the form of decorative or scented bouquets, dried lavender flowers can also be purchased from processors. Dried lavender flowers, although they do not contain essential oil anymore, keep all the aroma of this plant and can be used by manufacturers to give the typical scent of lavender to cosmetic products, room fragrances, and food products.

2- FLORAL COMPOSITIONS

Lavender is often used to embellish and perfume houses, terraces, gardens, stores, restaurants, and many other places. For this reason, it can be sold in the form of floral compositions, such as centerpieces and other compositions for ceremonies, or as potpourri, made of dried lavender flowers left to macerate for some time in essential oil. Country- and modern-themed weddings often require decorations with lavender as the protagonist, taking the thousand shades of this flower as the main colors, from the lightest lilac to the most intense blue. The lavender flower can perfectly adapt to several styles, a country one on the one hand, and a minimalist and modern one on the other, due to its exceptionally long and thin stems and its particular flower. Depending on one's imagination, you could create unique and original compositions responding to different needs.

3 - LAVENDER ESSENTIAL OIL

Also known as lavender aromatic essence, essential oil is a product obtained from lavender plants through distillation. Once extracted from the plant, the essential oil is liquid, dense, oily, and colorless. It is characterized by an intense aroma and can be used both pure and diluted as a personal perfume for body massages, to perfume rooms and linens, for aromatic baths, and in whirlpool baths, steam baths, saunas, inhalations with beneficial effects on the respiratory system, and much more.

When cooking, you may also use lavender essential oil to aromatize dishes at the end of cooking or add some to cakes and pies before starting to cook them. Lavender essential oil is the base of many cosmetic and personal care products and has a very high resale ability in different sectors. Given its many uses, many customers and end-users, especially girls and women, are curious to try its beneficial properties of aromatic lavender essence at home and take advantage of this magnificent, scented elixir. It will also be possible to offer oneself as a supplier of lavender essential oil to various processing activities. Finally, you should consider that processors will sell essential oil in large quantities while retailers should prefer ¼, ¾, 1 ½, and 3 ¼-oz packs.

4 - LAVENDER HYDROLAT

During the distillation of lavender, two substances are formed: the essential oil and the hydrolat. If essential oils, as we have seen, are the substances that, most of all, contain the properties and benefits of the plant, aromatic waters obtained through the distillation of medicinal plants, more simply called hydrolats, preserve many of these properties, even if in lower concentrations. The main difference between the two products is that while essential oils are concentrated in water-soluble compounds, hydrolats are concentrated in fat-soluble ones. Therefore, hydrolats are frequently used in cosmetics as an aqueous base, although not infrequently also used pure, directly on the skin, alone or mixed. Hydrolats are excellent tonics that are useful to refresh the skin, remove impurities, and decongest. They are also widely used as aromatizers. The existing customer segments for hydrolat are very similar to that of essential oil.

5 - POTTED PLANTS

Another interesting product to sell is potted plants, which can be purchased by the customer to be transplanted in a garden or agricultural land, even for ornamental purposes. Due to potted plants' different purposes, it is important that the grower highlights the properties of the species of lavender or potted plants for sale, and its uses in various fields, so that the customer can make a transparent and informed purchase. Therefore, clients, garden designers, flower stores, or various commercial activities or restaurants that want to beautify their outdoor spaces can be interested in trying their hands at gardening. To promote the good health of the lavender plant, you may add to the package a fertilizer or bag of soil to use while transplanting, and why not, a small instruction manual for the proper cultivation of the plant. Nowadays, it is possible to sell plants online and quickly deliver in many parts of the world with recyclable paper packages. On an online shop, there can be plants of different sizes and various species of lavender, so consider accurately describing the properties and specific needs of each of them.

6 - CUTTINGS

Cuttings are the lateral shoots of the plant, cut during the summer to be transplanted in a pot and then, once rooted, in the ground.

The propagation method for cuttings is the most common for lavender plants and the only one to allow lavandin plants, as a hybrid species that does not produce seeds, to reproduce. Therefore, the cuttings of lavandin will be very sought after as they are fundamental for the propagation of this species.

Cuttings can be stored in the dark and left to dry for two to three days. Until their sale, they will need to be stored in special containers with a suitable rooting compound and, likewise, sold with natural rooting hormones, which help the root development.

Individuals wishing to grow a new plant in a pot and farms desiring to start cultivation will be interested in buying cuttings. In both cases, the buyer will reserve them in advance and purchase them during the planting period. The cuttings can be packed and sold in single plastic bags or, if they must undergo a long shipment, wrapped in sheets of paper and protected by polystyrene boxes.

7 - SEEDS

Seeds of Lavandula latifolia can be sold, like cuttings, to those who already cultivate this plant or those who have decided to start their cultivation from scratch. Let us remember that the hybrid species of lavender does not produce seeds. Seeds of lavender can be sold in handy plastic or paper bags, which report, on the back, a little description of the periods and the proper way of sowing. With seeds only, you can make fascinating products, such as greeting cards made from recycled paper that can be planted and grow into a beautiful lavender plant. Although seeds have a more specific sale ability and usability, they can still be a source of side income.

8 - POTTING SOIL AND FERTILIZERS

The farm can sell potting soils and fertilizers that are ideal for the excellent growth of lavender and lavandin to customers wishing to repot or interplant seedlings optimally at home. The potting soil, dry and clayey, and organic fertilizers, with the right concentration of phosphorus, nitrogen, potassium, iron, magnesium, zinc, and copper, can be packed in bags of 5, 13, or 21 gallons and resold to dealers or individuals who try their hands at this type of cultivation.

9 - DIY CULTIVATION KITS

Today, DIY and indoor cultivation are very much in vogue, along with the rediscovery of a movement that admires and follows the rhythms of nature. Thus, some farms have created original kits for cultivation for those who want to test themselves and take care of their plants from birth. These kits are packages containing one or more lavender or lavandin cuttings, along with all the necessary tools for repotting and managing the plant. It can be, for example, plastic or terracotta pots of different diameters, specific potting soils, fertilizers, and instruction booklets for the right grafting and subsequent care for the proper growth of the plant, such as pruning and positioning inside or outside. The kit's price varies according to the variety of the cutting, the age of the original plant, and the number of accessories. This is a captivating idea to promote online, accompanied by all the benefits that a lavender plant entails, thus finding a relatively large market.

10 - GIFT BASKETS AND PACKS

With the products on sale in the business, you can make many original and impactful gift packages. One of the most typical solutions is to create a case, box, or small basket that contains some of the best-selling products of the company, such as, a potted plant of lavender and some bags of dried and fresh flowers. The basket can be more varied if made in collaboration with processing companies. In this case, you can also add food, cosmetics, room fragrances, and more. Baskets and packages can be sold all year round and be customized according to the season and major holidays. For it to be a success, you must also pay attention to the packages' aesthetic. If the cultivation is configured as organic, it could be profitable to underline the genuineness of the product by proposing only packages made of ecological materials.

Moreover, the baskets can be a very welcomed gift and an incentive for those who visit the lavender grove or buy other products. Sending completely organic and ecological baskets to Instagram influencers and YouTubers who share similar interests can represent an excellent source of profitable advertising. In addition, they can be distributed in local stores, accompanied by business cards and informational brochures to gain visibility in the area.

11 - PRODUCTS DERIVED FROM LAVENDER PROCESSING

As an integration of income, you can freely decide to sell a series of products — food and non-food — based on the precious lavender cultivated in an autonomous, organic, and "0-mile" way. This is an option if the company deals with both the cultivation and processing of lavender. However, even if it does not directly provide for the processing of raw materials, depending on the products, you can still agree to produce these products with lavender cultivation with small businesses, processors, and companies working for third parties.

Countless products can be made with lavender. They branch out in different categories, such as food, phytotherapy, aromatherapy, beauty, house-cleaning products, decorations, and even products dedicated to pets. All these preparations are effortless to implement. The company should provide a section that deals with these artisan productions. Their being handmade, completely organic, 0-mile, natural, and beneficial will attract a good audience.

Lavender, in all these fields, is used because of its intrinsic properties, such as:

- Antibacterial properties in products intended for cleaning the house
- Relaxing properties, as far as aromatherapy is concerned
- Calming effect. When used on irritated and sensitive skin, lavender feels gentle and regenerating
- Anti-odor properties, as lavender erases any odor in the pets kennel and fur
- A better night's sleep when sprinkled on a pillow
- Refreshing properties when sprinkles on linens and drawers
- Beautiful aesthetics, making it ideal for arrangements to keep in the home.

LAVENDER BASED FOODS - SOME IDEAS

Although lavender is thought to be more suited for perfuming closets and rooms, in reality, there also are many uses for it in the food sector. From honey to cheese, from cookies to preserves, and from chocolate to syrups and liqueurs, lavender gives a taste and flavor to a wide variety of foods.

The cheeses that are best associated with the lavender flavor are mainly sheep and goat aged cheeses, ideal on toasted bread, together with vegetable preserves, honey, and sweet and sour compotes, or simply grated on first and second courses and, of course, accompanied with an excellent fruity wine. Lavender, so fresh and scented, will give the cheese a delicate and particular taste.

Sauces, pâtés, and creams are more or less dense creamy preparations, ideal for flavoring every kind of dish, giving them a unique and inimitable taste. The use of creams and pâtés offers a wide range of opportunities, from the garnishing of sandwiches to the accompaniment of typical cheeses, braised and boiled meats, but also a condiment. Lavender sauces, creams, and pâtés can be packaged and sold in medium-sized glass jars or tin-plated metal cans. Sweetening tea and herbal teas with delicious lavender-flavored sugar can provide a unique and intoxicating sensory experience. For its preparation, you can use classic white caster sugar or whole cane sugar. Then, add dried lavender flowers and leave them to rest in a hermetically sealed container for about a week, shaking it from time to time to distribute lavender essential oils better. Lavender sugar can be packaged in glass bottles with a cork stopper or hermetic closure. The particularity of flavored jams makes them ideal for a gastronomic, tasty, and original gift. Many producers have chosen to experiment with new recipes to make flavored jams and marmalades or tasting jams, enriched by spices, aromatic herbs, and dried fruits. These jams can be made with one or more fruits and, often, keep small pieces of fruits inside. The inspiration for these preparations comes from chutneys, sweet and sour or spicy sauces used to accompany traditional Indian dishes. With lavender, you can make many types of flavored fruit jams, from the most traditional ones to the least common ones. For example, apple, pear, peach, raspberry, fig, rosehip, or elderberry jam, all naturally flavored with the fresh aroma of lavender. You may sell original dark, milk, or white chocolate bars as well as delicious chocolates and pralines flavored with lavender from the farm. Chocolates, excellent with dessert wines and grapes, but also in flakes on delicious cheeses, and perfect for preparing other sweets, will be packed in transparent paper, aluminum foil, or straw paper.

Combining acacia or wildflower honey with lavender essence offers food with an irresistible taste that perfectly matches with cheeses with strong and robust flavors. Moreover, this honey has remarkable anti-inflammatory, calming, and depurative properties.

Making cookies made of "00" flour, sugar, fresh eggs, butter, yeast, lavender, and other delicious ingredients such as toasted hazelnuts, chocolate nuggets, or raisins can also be an excellent idea to allow clients to taste lavender in the form of a cake, possibly paired with a delicate infusion. Lavender-flavored cookies can be sold in cardboard or tin packages, as well as in personalized glass jars. In addition to cookies, you can offer other types of lavender-based desserts. For instance, you can make cake bases, such as sponge cake and shortcrust pastry, or spoon desserts, such as panna cotta and custard. But not only! Indeed, lavender can be used to give a unique taste to other bakes, such as bread, breadsticks, and salty brioches, to name a few. Of course, it is better to choose ingredients as natural and organic as possible, buy from safe suppliers, and maybe prefer a vegetal alternative to the ingredients described above. In this way, those who follow a vegan diet will be able to approach this type of preparation. By dissolving lavender powder in milk and cream, you can make delicious lavender ice cream with an unusual and particular aroma. The ice cream can then be sold on the refrigerator counters, in jars or plastic tubs. On the package, you may print advice on how to serve and combine lavender ice cream, for example, with a drizzle of caramel on top, sprinkled chopped almonds, chocolate granules, etc.

An ancient use of lavender, although still in demand, is for the preparation of hot drinks, in which it appears tasty and rich in beneficial properties. Herbal teas, infusions, and decoctions are an aqueous extraction of the active principles present in the lavender plant, that is phytotherapeutic preparations containing essential oils, vitamins, minerals, and trace elements. The lavender plant is in fact known for its calming and relaxing properties. Lavender herbal teas and infusions can be sold in bags of various weights or disposable sachets. Finally, by combining a soft, high fermentation beer made with hops, barley malt, and wheat with lavender powder or extract, we obtain a medium alcoholic beverage with a characteristic amber-blonde color and the typical aroma of lavender, ideal to accompany fresh and light dishes.

LAVENDER SUPPLEMENTS

To make supplements, you will need more scientific knowledge. Due to its calming and relaxing properties, lavender essential oil is indeed also used to make dietary supplements. To do so, you may evaluate the collaboration with a local manufacturing company, which will be provided with the raw material from which the beneficial active principles will be extracted and used to make the food supplements. If the cultivation also deals with the distillation, the essential oil can be delivered directly to the processing company.

The supplements can be made, at the discretion of the owner of the cultivation and the producer, in tablets or powder to be diluted in warm water. Lavender has beneficial effects for those who suffer from sleep disorders and relaxes the body and mind.

In addition, its effects help with headaches and daily stress. This is why lavender supplements know a wide success, both locally and online.

PERSONAL CARE PRODUCTS

The soothing and calming properties of lavender oil include a panacea for skin and hair care, which appear visibly nourished and healthier. For this reason, you can propose soaps for the face and hands, bath foam, and shampoo made with lavender oil. By adding other ingredients of natural origins to the lavender essential oil, you can obtain specific soaps and detergents for every type of skin. For example, lavender and clay soap is ideal for impure skins, while lavender and calendula soap work wonders for sensitive skins, lavender and lotus flower soap is emollient, and lavender and bran soap is smoothing. Meanwhile, you can sell shampoo and shower gel in the form of solid soaps — instead of liquid soaps sold in classic plastic packaging — to further respect the environment and use the zero-waste practice. The soaps can then be wrapped in reusable wax paper, and shampoos and liquid soaps can be sold in glass jars, which are much more environmentally friendly than plastic containers since they can be recycled.

LAVENDER BEAUTY PRODUCTS

Lavender can be used for beauty products for its relaxing and calming properties, making it an excellent base for the realization of natural and beneficial cosmetics. Several products can be proposed, from day and night face creams, to gels and creams for the body and hands, to lipsticks and sunscreens. In particular, lavender-based after-sun creams are highly effective in calming and soothing sunburns. Besides, do not forget about the perfumes and fragrances for the body, fresh, and intoxicating, as well as the delicate and enveloping massage oils, all offered in meticulous packaging. Usually, lavender body butter and lotions are prepared with cocoa butter, coconut oil, or shea butter. These moisturizers help nourish the skin, while lavender gives off its aroma and relaxes the body and mind.

HOUSEHOLD CLEANING PRODUCTS

The characteristic scent of lavender is now also widely used to give detergents and household cleaning products a fresh and pleasant aroma. Starting from the raw material of the cultivation, you can make arrangements with local processing companies to produce lavender-based liquid detergents for the floor, sprays for the surfaces of the whole house, and sanitizers for the bathroom floor. Lavender's scent is also excellent as a detergent for all surfaces, and bags of lavender buds can be used as a refresher for clothes in the dryer.

PRODUCTS FOR THE ENVIRONMENT

Finally, the aesthetic and aromatic characteristics of the lavender flower easily lend themselves to the creation of ornamental decor and objects for room scenting. You may sell lavender-scented bags to be kept in drawers or closets, potpourris, centerpieces, candles, room diffusers, scented sprays, and much more. The success of all these products is linked to their presentation, so even when creating ornaments, you need to be very original.

CHAPTER 11
BEST SERVICES TO OFFER

Besides selling the agricultural products of the cultivation and those made from lavender, you can diversify the offer of the activity with some services, such as guided tours of the cultivation to allow those who are curious to learn about every aspect of life at a lavender field, from planting to distillation. The activity's primary services range from online sales to the organization of guided tours of the cultivation, to dedicated workshops and training courses. Once a business has acquired a considerable online presence and a good reputation, it can offer technical advice on how to best grow lavender. In addition, the service or product creation can deal with gadgets for corporate events or ceremonies, books on lavender, and raising awareness on issues such as biodiversity and environmental sustainability. The lavender grove is surprisingly beautiful, especially in the spring and when in full bloom. For this reason, it could lend itself as an exceptional location for photoshoots and videos or special events. The possibilities of earning money through lavender cultivation are more numerous than you might think. Those are divided between the company's ability to be recognizable and present online using a solid marketing strategy, and to be present in the territory to be found physically and establish relationships with more locals.

ONLINE SALE
To open an e-commerce is to open yourself to infinite options. Always being on the web, managing communication through blogs, websites, social media, and more brings multiple advantages, including the possibility to reach a potentially unreachable audience, communicate with customers, be found both virtually and physically. By focusing on the organization of a "virtual showcase," an e-commerce with constantly updated lists of available products, described in detail and attractively and accompanied with the

relevant prices and delivery times, can integrate direct sales and expand its catchment area. If you decide to sell plants and cuttings, make sure the transport system is efficient and fast. Moreover, to ensure the high quality of the products, it is preferable to offer a booking service for plants, cuttings, and seeds so that the products are shipped at the right time, in terms of season and maturity. Although the online sale is not the only way to earn money, we advise you to take care of the online presence of your activity so that you can be easily found. Besides, establishing relationships with locals on social media can be very useful as it feeds the spread of word of mouth. In any case, people in the area can see the products and choose to come and buy them directly on-site or come admire the beauty of the lavender field.

GUIDED TOURS AND WORKSHOPS

Guided tours allow customers to visit the lavender plantation with an expert who can explain its characteristics, cultivation methods, and main benefits. Depending on the area of the activity, you may also offer guided tours to school groups, tourists passing by, and residents who want to take the opportunity of learning about lavender, its properties, and its possible uses.

On the other hand, workshops mainly aim at hobbyists interested in learning the characteristics and methods of cultivation of this plant and its many uses, whether culinary, medical, or cosmetic. Unlike guided tours, workshops do not necessarily have to take place in the cultivation area but can be set up more comfortably in the farm buildings. For guided tours and workshops to be successful, getting the participants involved and promoting the initiative with the proper means is essential. For example, you could create educational materials to distribute to participants, such as small handouts or brochures. Depending on the intensity of the agricultural work and staff availability, you may either give tours on the weekends or during the week.

TRAINING COURSES AND PERSONALIZED ADVICE FOR NEW CROPS

The training courses, which can be intended for groups of growers or organized in individual lessons, are aimed at those who would like to set up a lavender crop to make an income or integrate the production of this plant in their agricultural activity and directly in the field. These courses can also be offered online through a simple PC and with tools dedicated to distance learning, such as Zoom, Microsoft Teams, Skype, and much more platforms.

During the courses, the grower can illustrate the cultivation techniques used, harvesting, selection of cuttings, distillation, and drying of flowers, to name a few. You can organize training courses on several days, like 10-to-15-hour seminars, or concentrate the didactic phase in one day or a weekend since the participants in the training courses could come from far away. In addition, the grower will be able to offer targeted and personalized advice for the creation of a new lavender or lavandin plantation, focusing on the difference between the species and the different uses that can be made of them. Personalized advice is a very marketable and profitable service. For example, you could open social groups dedicated to lavender growing and provide your knowledge to those who request it, or join dedicated online forums and acquire visibility.

PROCESSING WORKSHOP

Among the extra services that can be offered, customers will very much appreciate the realization of favors and other gadgets ideal for corporate gifts (and customized according to the customer's needs), such as glass cruets with lilac lavender flowers, fabric bags with powdered lavender, and wooden boxes containing whole or powdered lavender flowers. The culinary processing workshop could be an alternative. Indeed, creating lavender honey, lavender cheese, chocolates, tea, and ice cream could be a rewarding and exciting activity for many, as could be creating lavender-derived wellness and personal care products. You could also record eye-catching video recipes to post on social media, YouTube, or Pinterest to entice people to try making their own products and make themselves a name.

ADOPT A LAVENDER PLANT (or row)

In the farming domain, a rapidly growing trend is to offer customers the adoption of a plant (or, in the case of farms, an animal) that can be followed from a distance by its "owner" throughout all the phases of growth until its harvest. The cultivation can, therefore, propose its clients to "adopt a lavender plant/row." The payment of the (monthly or yearly) adoption fee by the customer will allow them to contribute to the care of their lavender plant and, after the harvest, get delivered some products made with its flowers. It is a service indicated during the last period that raises awareness on environmental issues. This type of service is also perfect as a gift. Indeed, customers can then give a lavender plant for adoption to those who love to take care of the environment and are attentive to issues of sustainability and ecology.

THIRD-PARTY SERVICE

Finally, supposing the cultivation also takes care of lavender processing, the distillation of the flowers is the first step to obtain the essential oil. In that case, the business can offer to act as a third-party processing company to all the other cultivations that do not possess a processing laboratory. This service will increase the company's revenue by using its equipment and, therefore, without having to invest in other machinery. On the other hand, before offering the service on behalf of third parties, you must ensure that you can support a more significant workload without it affecting the primary activity of your cultivation.

PHOTOSHOOTS AND WEDDINGS

A lavender field itself is a spectacle for the eyes, especially when in bloom, in the spring and summer until early September/October. For this reason, its beauty can encourage people to use it for both personal and corporate exceptional photoshoots, music videos, commercials, and films. Many artists who paint on canvas could also come to your lavender grove to portray the beauty of the colors and flowers. If your business has suitable premises, you could even host ceremonies, such as weddings and parties in general. All you need to do is hire a caterer, provide table settings, and the necessary options depending on the event. It could also be interesting to host and provide local fashion or automotive brands with a lavender purple backdrop for advertisements against a fee.

CHAPTER 12
FREE AND LOW-COST MARKETING TIPS

Thanks to the advances of the digital revolution and online marketing, it's now much easier to get your name out there and spread the word. In addition to classic advertising campaigns in local magazines, video spots, websites, and e-commerce, it is now possible to reach a broad audience that may potentially be interested in the cultivation of lavender and buying the products or services of the lavender farm in a way wholly free, or in some cases, at low cost. What you need in such cases is care and attention. It is indeed necessary to build a team of a couple or more people who can take care of the image of the activity. For example, rely on professional photographers to take pictures in the processing workshop, lavender field, premises, and of the people and different species. Sometimes, it is enough for the professional to visit the lavender field a couple of times a month to get an excellent service composed of photos or videos expendable on the web. The same goes for the graphic: a good graphic of the website, social pages, and images to post is essential to create and take care of the image of the activity. But, there also are many other inspiring and almost free ways to be found and recognized on the web and to differentiate yourself from potential competitors.

For a well-rooted, local lavender farm, social networks are valuable for its growth. Thus, ensure your brand's online presence relies on a zero-cost effective method to increase your chances of being found and enticing users to turn to your garden to purchase products or services. In this case, Google My Business probably the best web tool for a local business, becomes a crucial secret weapon as it allows you to geolocate your company on the web and appear both in searches and on Google Maps.

GOOGLE MY BUSINESS AND ITS ADVANTAGES FOR A LOCAL BUSINESS

A Google My Business tab is an extraordinary opportunity to display valuable information to potential customers in one place, such as:

- Information of contact
- Geolocation
- Opening hours
- Photos
- Reviews

Each of these individual activities helps improve the company's ranking on the internet and its visibility at no cost by generating more revenue. Increasing the relevance of your laundry on the internet will offer the concrete possibility to appear in the users' searches. We have to take into account that the users looking for local information are really into a purchasing funnel, and a fast and intuitive finding tool will confirm them that your lavender farm is the one that meets their needs and requirements. Several official estimates show that 50% of users who conduct a local search actually visit the store they are looking for within a day.

Not taking these factors into account means neglecting a crucial part of the market, losing potential customers, and decreasing sales. Google My Business provides significant advantages over all other marketing strategies as it does not require any specific basic skills, is entirely free, and has great return potential with minimal effort. A platform like Google My Business allows you to precisely geo-localize thanks to a tab on Google Maps and appear on Local Packs and Knowledge Local Panels. Let's see in detail what these are.

• Local Packs. Thanks to this free tool made available to companies by Google, it will be possible to appear in web searches within the Local Pack. This feature puts local companies close to users directly in the search results.

• Knowledge Local Panel. This feature is available for companies with an adequately created GMB tab and that have a certain degree of seniority. It aims to simplify user searches with a quick preview on the right side of the web screen.

• Google My Business tabs are a very effective free service for businesses that want to increase sales exponentially without investing money.

SOCIAL NETWORKS AN INDISPENSABLE RESOURCE

Why using social networks as platforms and showcases can be an effective strategy? Official estimates that more and more people are surfing social media in this hyper-connected, modern society.

● Instagram counts one billion monthly active users, making it the perfect ally for a laundry.

● Facebook counts more than twice as many and peaks at nearly two billion monthly active users.

Proper management of these and other extremely valuable platforms to a business like a lavender field, including YouTube, Pinterest, and many others can provide a real advantage over the competition and help generate traffic and sales. Local businesses can especially benefit from an active presence on social media as it provides them with several other benefits, such as those listed below.

● They are free. You don't need a dedicated budget to start building your social network.

● They increase the opportunities for direct contact with your audience. With those, you can provide valuable content and use effective communication to build audience loyalty with real sales benefits.

● They are an indispensable showcase. Having a virtual space accessible from anywhere and to anyone is an infallible method of getting the brand's name out there.

● They can be a source of passive income. By patiently growing your online presence with quality content, you may eventually earn from the views and collaboration opportunities that will spontaneously open up for the lavender farm.

● They allow you to study. At first glance, it may not seem important, but analyzing the data that social networks offer means learning to know your users in-depth and concretely.

PRACTICAL INSTRUCTIONS FOR USING SOCIAL NETWORKS TO YOUR ADVANTAGE

Throughout all platforms, you must be able to distinguish your communication from that of all your competitors. Copywriting must not simply aim at quantity but also quality. Therefore, it is necessary to provide an initial plan to have an editorial calendar in mind that considers a fixed and constant presence that offers valuable content and quality for its possible customers.

Creating emotionally engaging content that manages to share the brand's specific voice is essential to foster all the metrics that distinguish the success of a company, including:

- Shares, comments, and likes
- Mentions
- Followers
- The use of the company's hashtags by other users.

To do this, studying the data provided by the platforms is the right way to engage in communication that feels personal — knowing your audience means using the right tone to engage them. Therefore, talking about one's brand is not helpful and not enough. To make a difference, the business will have to produce valuable, unique content that corresponds to several specifications:

- Address the possible concerns or questions of those interested in lavender cultivation and the processing of its products.
- Take the audience's unique needs into account.
- Have some imagination and creativity.

On social media, the company will have to simultaneously maintain two different types of attitudes, depending on the amount of time that can be devoted to one or more social platforms. It should be:

- Reactive. Respond to comment questions, mentions, and interact with your followers.
- Active. Many successful businesses spontaneously interact with their users without waiting to have to react.

A local business does not need to have a profile or page on all social networks, but it does need to maintain a constant presence on some of them. Diversified, mediocre, and sporadic communication will only waste time. Each social network offers specific content because each channel reaches different customer segments with varying spans of attention, ages, and social locations. Determining which social platform is best suited to keep your company's voice intact and offer a consistent presence is the best way to generate conversions and revenue from social media. For a lavender cultivation, some of the best platforms may be Pinterest, Instagram, YouTube, and Facebook.

PINTEREST

Pinterest is an interesting showcase as users are looking for inspiration there. Thus, you should use beautiful photos of the sink, finished products, and presenting recipes and creative ideas to draw people's attention and generate traffic to your website. Many people actively search for products' photos, giving numerous possibilities to explore the creativity inherent in those who will manage the social platform. On Pinterest, you can also use hashtags that link to a general description of the content and insert links that take users to the product or service pages of your lavender farm.

INSTAGRAM

On this platform, companies address a young and dynamic audience that gives lots of importance to the visual part of a post. That is why emotional communication, with beautiful, carefully studied photos will be effective. Looking for hashtags is also really important as these contribute to telling a story accurately. Reels and Stories are top-rated tools and allow you to share moments of the day or key updates in a way that seems to be in real-time to help shape the communication with your audience more directly and engagingly. Overall, this platform allows local businesses like laundries to implement fascinating microblogging strategies.

A few rules of thumb:

- On Instagram, you will need to consistently post on your feed at least once per day and publish at least two stories or reels.

- Exploit the industry's hashtags and create at least two or three of your own to intercept a wider audience. They should always be used in posts and the variation should be minimal.

YOUTUBE

On YouTube, you could upload videos that can grab the attention of those interested in lavandin activities. In many cases, what matters on this platform is to have a creative idea and carry it through. Unlike what it may seem, many users are willing to watch even very long videos if the topic interests them.

To fully take advantage of YouTube's benefits:

- Produce videos of emotional landscapes of the lavender field in bloom.

- Suggest interesting lavender recipes.

- Share tips on growing and preparing a plot.

- Make a vlog that tells the story of life on the farm.

- Show behind-the-scenes footage of lavender processing.

- Promote other businesses' services and products with effective storytelling. Give them visibility by offering them a space for photoshoots, collaborations, and ceremonies.

These are just some of the things you can do with a YouTube channel.

Some practical rules:

- The most active users manage to post a video per day, but on YouTube, even one per week is acceptable.

- On this platform, you can allow users to contribute to the costs related to maintaining the business through a subscription to your channel or by simply leaving the channel during a live or letting them watch a certain video as much as they want.

- Responding to comments and questions below the videos is important to build a relationship with your target audience.

FACEBOOK

This platform remains the most used platform within the social landscape, which is why a presence on it can be attractive. Facebook allows ample opportunities to maneuver with the creation of Business Pages and more. On there, building lead generation and conversions can be straightforward if you create valuable content capable of integrating images, videos, and text. Textual communication on Facebook can be broader and can allow for the construction of more articulated storytelling.

You must keep the broad audience in mind and maintain communication that goes straight to the point and cuts out all the superfluous. It is also essential that you use Call for Action in your posts that invite your audience's response. On Facebook, you can also join groups with specific interests or create your own. Doing so is a great way to share interesting content that will grow the brand's name. In this case, staying active within the community with answers, questions, and various types of interactions is very important.

Some rules of thumb:

- On Facebook, you should publish at least three posts per week.

- Focus on stories that can engage your audience, for instance through questions, questionnaires, and more.

- The platform is very attentive and performs a specific ranking. Posts with superlatives or positive nature have more chances to be seen by your audience.

INFLUENCER MARKETING

Influencers are personalities with a large audience of active followers on social media, who can significantly influence the public's purchasing decisions thanks to three distinctive characters:

- Authority. Users follow influencers because they recognize in them a certain authority of advice and trust their judgment.

- Knowledge. An influencer succeeds in winning over their target audience based on the knowledge they demonstrate about one or more niches, often collateral.

- Relationship with their target audience, that is, a distinct and substantial niche with which the influencer has created a point of contact and actively interacts.

In addition to acting as fundamental tools at the service of corporate marketing, influencers are an added value since they can establish social relationships thanks to which brands can collaborate to obtain substantial economic returns. Sometimes, influencers reach the same niche audience as the one companies want to reach, and for this reason, act as a link between the business and their target audience. Building a relationship between a brand and consumers is not an easy task. To achieve a successful and effective relationship, a company needs a thorough strategy that takes into account the data of the target audience and aims to establish a deeper and more stable multi-directional communication that listens to what users have to say and what they need. To easily reach most people within your industry, using someone who already has authority within that niche and establish partnerships is a suitable method. Doing so will increase the user base and audience and represent a decision-making turnaround within the company's marketing strategy.

OWNING A BLOG

A blog is meaningful for a company as it allows you to create valuable content for your customers. In this way, you can let them know about your lavender farm, push them to purchase your products or services, and present yourself as a symbol of quality. Whether linked to an e-commerce or not, a blog is a way to intercept people interested in the topic discussed. With a blog, you will be able to exploit the right keywords to build a reference scheme that allows you to appear in the first searching pages for free. It is the ideal space to tell your story, where you come from, and the goals and ideals of your company. Storytelling is essential to engage people, so tell them about your love for lavender, its indispensable uses in every area of daily life, and its many benefits.

A blog is a space that also allows you to use your own voice, without homologating, simply by responding to the fundamental dictates of writing for the web, including a minimum length of 600 words per post, short sentences with many points, lists and trivia that can attract more people, paying attention to the descriptions of images, and using keywords specific to your industry.

With a blog, you can:

- Retain customers and make them part of a project, news, and what happens in the company daily
- Sponsor your own activities, such as labs and workshops, by sharing experiences and participants' comments and feedback
- Propose free content that helps address particular needs and generates brand awareness
- Increase SEO and local SEO
- Produce specific content to disseminate via social media, such as recipes, valuable tips, FAQs, explanatory photos and videos, and more
- Expand the possibilities for sharing the brand's voice, making it unique and different from all the others.

A blog also encourages users to share opinions and passions, allows you to expand the possibilities of product sales, generate earnings through related product sponsorships, and do lead generation by building mailing lists and more.Before writing a blog post, you must conduct detailed research of the best keywords, using useful online tools such as:

- Google AdWords
- Ubersuggest

ANSWER THE PUBLIC

Remember that keywords, as well as flowers, respond to seasonal, regional, thematic prerogatives. Sometimes, even those of competitors can be useful. Keywords are words or phrases that respond to a direct need of the target audience. They help websites, e-commerce, and blogs be well-indexed in search engine rankings. If you offer content on the company blog, always answer potential users' questions clearly and concisely, and then detail the information.

A few rules of thumb:

- Make sure to publish consistent content.

- Make sure to structure your content consistently.

- You can end each article with a specific call to action that refers to a service you intend to sell. With such, it will be possible to book the service directly with one click.

CHAPTER 13
HOW TO DIFFERENTIATE FROM COMPETITORS

The first way to differentiate yourself within a market is to do the necessary market research by wondering which are the main competitors of the sink. You can identify them based on the products you choose to offer:

- Fresh or dried lavender

- Essential oils

- Food products

- Lavender-based cosmetics

- Lavender seeds

- Potted plants

Another very important aspect will be the sales methods and channels the company chooses to use. Exploring the territory and getting to know the competition is the only way to differentiate your offer. To do this, you can use a simple technique, such as SWOT analysis, to assess the strengths and weaknesses of your company within the market. It is a key aspect to maximizing sales, neutralizing incidents before they can even happen, and leveraging your business's strengths.

The acronym **SWOT** stands for:

● **Strengths**. It indicates precisely what your organization's strengths are so you can understand how it stands out from other players on the market. For example, the lavender production processes or widespread local exposure might be one of your strengths. To find out your strengths, wonder what your company does better than others, and what unique resources it has. By knowing this, you will know the market.

• **Weaknesses**. Honestly assessing the weaknesses of a business allows you to contain them, keep potential flaws under control, and turn them, with inventiveness and ingenuity, into real strengths. Identify the vulnerabilities, think about what could be avoided and what needs to be improved, and you will have an advantage on your target market.

• **Opportunities**. Finding the right niche, evaluating the opportunities within the market that no competitor has identified or been able to exploit yet means acquiring a vast pool of potential buyers. So, evaluate market trends, the potential direction of a local policy on agriculture or nutraceuticals, for example. Sometimes, all it takes is a small opportunity, such as a minimal change in social models or in the behavior of the public, to allow those who know how to seize it to increase their competitiveness. It's not a question of rewriting the game's rules but of learning how to apply them well.

• **Threats**. What are the external threats to the company? It's critical to anticipate threats in the medium to long term and act preemptively so that the market doesn't overtake you. Consider what your competitors are developing, assess whether or not there may be problems with supply, planting or harvesting, and constantly monitor the market.

Once this analysis has been carried out, you must not let what you have discovered remain on paper but transform this long list into an operational plan. To do so:

- Focus on your strengths and cut investments where they are not helpful.

- Try to diversify without taking away your uniqueness.

- Carry all the options that have been generated and apply them on a practical level in the company and on the ground.

Once you've completed the market research, you will finally possess the data to understand what differentiates your business from competitors and you can use those differences to manage adversity.

Assessing the competition in your target market by making a clear distinction about it is a very effective way to identify strengths, opportunities, weaknesses, and dangers for your business. A plausible distinction is:

- Herbalists, perfumeries and pharmacies.

- Retail stores selling organic or local products.

- Other local producers.

- Nurseries, garden centers, and flower stores.
- Online businesses.

Let's take a detailed look at what assessments can be made after proper market segmentation.

HERBALISTS, PERFUMERIES AND PHARMACIES

These activities can be both a source of opportunities and risks. They become possibly subject to exploitation when they open the chink to become suppliers of raw materials, but if they can produce their own raw materials and products derived from them, they must be viewed as competitors. An advantage a farmer has over these activities is its ability to offer organic and local products of certifiable quality, especially considering that many herbalists or pharmacies are supplied by foreign growers whose materials' quality is not always verifiable.

RETAIL STORES SELLING ORGANIC OR LOCAL PRODUCTS

This type of business, in the local market, can be used as a springboard for your company. In fact, over time, it will have educated the consumer to a presence in the area of a particular type of organic and local products, thus providing an excellent starting point for a grower who wants to promote their business to the general public. Retail stores are also often on the lookout for zero-mileage producers who can provide excellent value for money.

Suppose they enter into direct competition with the business. In that case, starting to check what products are being sold and offering diverse choices at low prices and of low impact can be an effective way to differentiate yourself from these competitors.

OTHER LOCAL PRODUCERS

These activities often offer products applying the 0-mile principle, allowing customers to appreciate fresh, quality products. In this case, to differentiate from these specific competitors, you must focus on competitive prices and offering high-quality products. Exclusivity also plays in favor of the company as many buyers are willing to invest money in unique and quality products in this specific market niche. Another differentiation can be made about the target market. Indeed, offering what is not already provided by local companies will hit a virgin niche: food, supplements, organic cosmetics, and pharmaceuticals are all important and diversify the offer. In the end, you will have more products that will raise the total price of an average receipt. Let's take the example of a business that proposes products based on its lavender field and with its own food, cosmetic, and pharmaceutical products. If competing with other such companies, making the public aware of the existence of your brand, producing compelling storytelling, and letting final consumers in the area know the products offered and the business itself is a sure way to be appreciated by the market.

NURSERIES, GARDEN CENTERS, AND FLOWER STORES

Nurseries, garden centers, and flower stores can be direct competitors of your lavender field if they offer customers lavender seedlings, seeds, bouquets, and ornamental tools. With more accessibility and the ability to easily meet the public's needs, they may be preferred over a lavender production center. However, such businesses very often have a limited range of products to offer, as well as higher prices. Your business can, for example, use these features to reduce its prices by being directly involved in the production and providing a convenient home service that bypasses the problem of remoteness.

ONLINE ACTIVITY

Within the web's fabulous chaos, many platforms and websites sell every possible lavender product, from oils to cuttings to single plants. A direct grower can certainly fight on the same level by opening their showcase website and aiming at a high-quality, perfectly shipped product to counter the competition. Opening an e-commerce is very advantageous even though it can be a double-edged sword if you don't update your website and don't make attractive proposals.

FOUR PRACTICAL TIPS TO STAND OUT WITHIN THE MARKET

Once you know how to conduct effective market research that provides results on production efficiency, sales, and conversions, you must develop practical attitudes toward these methods.

That is why the four practical tips shown below, if put into practice, can offer excellent results.

1 - YOUR MESSAGE

A sure way to attract customers is through direct communication, and more specifically, a clear message. Focusing on the benefits you can bring to their lives is primordial and building a relationship with customers through the creation of quality content will allow your company to stand out. End-consumers want to know what your business can do for them, and this is also your secret weapon to play. Use compelling storytelling, come up with new ideas and updated products.

Find your own, personal and emotional way to recount what you do, and you will hold your business' success in your hands.

2 - EXPAND YOUR HORIZONS

Whenever possible, expanding into new market segments is a valuable idea. Differentiating your offerings leads to faster and better growth. Once you've assessed whether or not your launderette has a chance to expand its area of influence into collateral markets, do so decisively.

3 - PARTNERSHIPS

Establishing winning partnerships with local or digital customers, or a mix of both, is beneficial for both a young company and the more established ones. Being able to count on the power of innovation, both realities can benefit from the relationship, aspiring to ambitious goals deemed unattainable by themselves.

Today, both larger and smaller companies seize the opportunity of forming alliances to open up to different and varied market segments.

4 - TAKE CARE OF YOUR TEAM

A cohesive team that feels valued and has common goals is the real secret to success within any company or business. Find your own way of sharing enthusiasm and ideals with your team, by example, with excellent communication or incentives of various kinds. Whichever way you choose, do it!

Ensure that those who work for you know their jobs, are well-trained, and most importantly, want to go to work thanks to a stimulating environment.

+100 CRAFTS, HANDMADE GIFTS & NATURAL REMEDIES

AROMATHERAPY AND WELL-BEING

1- LAVENDER BATH SALTS

The Romans had already grasped the main qualities of this precious lavender flower and used to immerse themselves in thermal baths surrounded by the calming, relaxing, and regenerating scent of lavender while chatting meekly. Even today, you can repeat the ancient habit of taking things easy, lying in a warm tub and melting away all the tensions of the day.

INGREDIENTS
- 2 cups of sea salt
- 2 tablespoons of dried lavender buds
- 10 to 15 drops of lavender essential oil
- A few drops of lavender soap (optional)
- Food coloring as desired
- An airtight glass jar

PREPARATION
This recipe is effortless and only entails mixing the ingredients inside a large container. If you would like to obtain a product with different colors, divide the salts, either add food coloring or melted lavender soap in one of the containers, and mix.

Then, put the two salts in the glass jar, alternating them to create an aesthetically pleasing fantasy. The salts obtained should be closed and left to rest for a couple of days to give way to the aroma of lavender to infuse its benefits.

USAGE TIPS

Dissolve 3-4 tablespoons of bath salts and soak in a warm bathtub for 20 minutes. Lavender relieves fatigue and provides calm and tranquility. Moreover, the antiseptic and relaxing properties of lavender have been known for centuries. This plant with extraordinary effects is straightforward enough to even grow in pots on your balcony as it is a resistant plant that does not require much water.

These salts are not bad as a scrub either. In a small bowl, mix a couple of tablespoons of bath salts and the bath foam to taste. After that, gently rub the salts on the skin in circular motions to benefit from a gentle and relaxing exfoliation.

2 - LAVENDER SCENTED CANDLES

Suppose you are looking for a fresh and intense fragrance that can stimulate the senses and relax your mind and body. In that case, there is nothing better than a lavender candle that will spread its scent gradually and pleasantly throughout the room. The lavender candle is a charming and colorful ornament to keep in any room. However, a dried lavender does not spread its magnificent smell as quickly and evenly as a candle.

INGREDIENTS
- 2-3 pounds of candle wax
- ½ ounce of lavender essential oil
- Candle wicks
- Natural blue and red candle dye
- Glass jars
- Hot glue
- Food thermometer

PREPARATION

First of all, it is better to lay a newspaper or baking paper under the glass jars to prevent any leakage of the wax from causing damages to the surface onto which you work. Next, you must stick the base of the wicks with hot glue on the bottom of the glass jars chosen for the candles. The jars must be cleaned from remains of food or any other substance and dried well inside. Finally, make sure the wicks, which should be ¼ to ¾ inches higher than the top of the wax, are placed at the center of the jar.

Blend the candle wax in a double boiler. In this case, you need to choose an old pot or vessel to use exclusively for candle making and not for cooking. The wax should reach 180°F, after which you need to turn off the heat and let it cool down to 120°F and add ½ ounce of lavender essential oil for every 2-3 lbs. of wax. Now is the time to add the dye. To get a soft lavender color, you'll just need to mix blue and red candle dye in equal amounts.

To obtain the desired coloration, it is crucial to mix the colors a little at a time. Otherwise, it is impossible to reverse. It is not necessary to add lavender buds because they could catch on fire while the candle is burning, and also because the candle will already have an intoxicating scent. All you have to do now is pour the hot wax inside the jars.

USAGE TIPS

This recipe is easy to make by hand and requires very few ingredients. The jars can be reused for new candles once the prepared ones are finished, or you can decorate the lids and offer them as gifts to loved ones. What is certain is that you can take advantage of the relaxing properties of the lavender scent, which will be released evenly and gradually across the room. The candles are also a great gift if closed and decorated, perhaps using a label that describes lavender's properties.

3 - LAVENDER POTPOURRI

Lavender is a fragrance that can take your mind back in time and relax your body and spirit.

A potpourri is ideal to always have this aroma available in different corners of the house, maintaining a pleasant appearance, and above all, constantly providing the incredible sensory benefits of the lavender scent.

INGREDIENTS
- Dried lavender buds
- Lavender essential oil
- Cones
- Containers with caps

PREPARATION

Add as many drops as desired, based on how strong you want the potpourri to smell, to the dried lavender buds. Potpourri can be made from dried citrus peels and dried flower petals. You can either purchase some of these ingredients at a regular market or dry and add dried citrus fruits, such as oranges, grapefruits, lemons, and tangerines, by placing their peels on the heater during the winter. On the other hand, if you want to keep the lavender-only potpourri to reap all its anti-stress and calming benefits, you can mix the drops with the buds to spread the scent across all the buds. Even the simplest potpourri preparation will represent a relaxing practice that will immediately put you in a good mood.

USAGE TIPS

The ideal would be to keep the potpourri in a container that you can close, if necessary, and decorate as you wish. Add small pine cones to give it a more rustic touch. The potpourri may run out, which is why its scent should be renewed from time to time to keep the scent intense.

4- FRESH LAVENDER LEMONADE

Lavender lemonade is a thirst-quenching summer drink that is also fragrant and cleanses the body while lowering the daily stress caused by busy days. This easy-to-prepare, healthy drink satiates the palate and naturally keeps you cool during summer days. This relaxing and purifying lemonade can be kept in the fridge for days and is ideal to offer to thirsty guests.

INGREDIENTS
- 5 glasses of water
- The juice of 6 lemons
- 1-2 lavender sprigs
- 1 tablespoon of honey or the sweetener of your choice

PREPARATION

Carefully wash the fresh lavender sprigs and set them aside to dry. Put the water in a large pot and add the sprigs and the honey or other natural sweetener of your choice. Bring the mix to boil, and then, allow it to cool. Meanwhile, wash, cut, and squeeze the juice of six lemons, filtering it through a sieve to avoid collecting residue. The water with lavender must also be filtered and added to the lemon juice, and then, left to cool in the refrigerator for two to three hours, after which it will be ready to serve fresh.

As an alternative to lavender sprigs, you can prepare lemonade with 100% pure lavender essential oil for alimentary use. To do so, add 5 lemons and 1 drop of essential oil to ½ gallon of water. Honey can also be added as desired by mixing the ingredients while they're cold. This procedure reduces the time of preparation and provides a thirst-quenching, beneficial drink that is perfect to sip at sunset with friends as a relaxing aperitif.

USAGE TIPS
To make the lemonade a little fizzy, you may mix it with some sparkling wine for a sensational aperitif. Also, accompanying the lavender lemonade with a decorative lavender sprig makes it even more aesthetically pleasing while you get to spend some summertime with friends.

5- LAVENDER ANTI-STRESS BALL

Stress is now a daily reality with which we are accustomed to live. However, it is impossible to eliminate excess accumulations that can be harmful to health thanks to lavender. Nevertheless, its natural properties have powerful calming properties and guarantees satisfying results if combined with the power of an anti-physical stress ball.

INGREDIENTS
- 1 cup of flour
- 3 tablespoons of cream of tartar
- ½ cup of boiling water
- ½ cup of salt
- 1 tablespoon of oil
- 1 tablespoon of green food coloring
- 20 drops of lavender essential oil
- Glitter to taste

PREPARATION
Take a pot and put water to boil. Meanwhile, combine flour with the cream of tartar and a tablespoon of oil. Add the water and green food coloring, and

mix with your hands until the ingredients are thoroughly blended. Next, put in glitter to taste, starting with 2 tablespoons. Once you reach the desired consistency, add 20 drops of lavender essential oil and mix again.

USAGE TIPS
Using this stress reliever when you are feeling stressed really is a panacea. Giving off the intense scent of lavender will not only be helpful but also really calming and 100% natural. You will then have the opportunity to relax with an aromatherapy product that does not pollute. This product will last for up to two weeks, and you can moisten it with an atomizer if it is too dry.

6- LAVENDER NATURAL RELAXING BABY OIL

When you have a baby, taking care of them becomes a priority. Meeting their resting needs is vital, so helping them fight anxiety and stress and sleep deeply without using harmful products is of paramount importance. Lavender is a natural, non-harmful product that perfumes and calms thanks to its essences.

INGREDIENTS
- 3 cups of cold-pressed almond oil
- 1 tablespoon of dried lavender buds
- 1 bag of linen

PREPARATION
Take a glass jar and fill it with the 3 cups of almond oil. Then, take a linen bag and place the dried lavender buds in it. Soak the bag in the almond oil and place the glass jar inside a container half-full of water. Leave to infuse on low heat for 3 hours. Allow the oil to cool down and squeeze the bag to let the lavender essence release every last drop.

USAGE TIPS
Dip a wad of absorbent cotton inside the oil and gently apply it onto your baby's skin before putting them to bed. The lavender, with its intense smell, will help them relax and sleep deeply while the almond oil will keep their skin healthy and moisturized.

7- LAVENDER LINGERIE SPRAY

Bedtime after a long, busy day is a ritual that allows you to take care of yourself. Lavender is especially beneficial for those who suffer from sleep disorders or insomnia but is also perfect for those who simply want to relax at the end of the day. After a bath and after putting on comfortable clothes, slipping into linen or cotton sheets treated with lavender spray induces deep and relaxing sleep and the possibility to wake up relaxed and rested the next morning.

INGREDIENTS
- 4 tablespoons of dried lavender flowers
- 2 ½ cups of water
- Coffee filter
- Funnel
- 2 tablespoons of alcohol
- 12 drops of lavender essential oil
- Clean spray bottle

PREPARATION
Bring one cup of water with 4 tablespoons of dried lavender flowers to boil. Once boiling, remove it from the heat and infuse it as herbal tea. At this point, put the coffee filter in a funnel, pour the mixture, and let it cool in a jar, so it discards the lavender buds from the combination. Once the whole mix has been drained, you can remove the coffee filter. In another pot, bring another cup and a half of water to boil, remove from the heat, and add 12 drops of lavender essential oil and two tablespoons of alcohol to the mixture. Then, simply put the lid on the jar and shake vigorously.
Once the mixture has cooled down, it will be possible to put it into the dedicated spray bottle using the funnel. Then, all you have to do is use the lavender spray!

USAGE TIPS
Insomnia is a pretty recurring problem, and good restorative sleep is what we need for a healthy life. Sheets, and especially pillows, are primary elements for optimal sleep: lavender spray and a frequent change of linen allow you to relax thanks to lavender's ability to calm the anxiety and stress accumulated during the day.

8 - HERBAL PILLOW FOR HEADACHES

Tired eyes, stress, headaches, or difficulty sleeping are common conditions that do not allow you to rest optimally. In these cases, an herbal pillow indicated to infuse a profound relaxing and calming effect, both physical and mental, could help. What also works when using an herbal pillow is the weight of the rice on the eyes that physically soothes the pain.

At the same time, lavender's natural scent comes out and infuses an extraordinary calming effect.

INGREDIENTS

- Two pieces of 9.5 x 4.5-inch cotton, silk, or satin fabric
- 2/3 cup of rice or flaxseed
- 1/3 cup of dried lavender flowers

PREPARATION

To make this little headache pillow, you don't need much sewing knowledge. Instead, you only need to choose two equal pieces of fabric with a lovely pattern. Then, simply sew the edges of the fabrics together and leave a corner a couple of inches open, so you can flip the pillow and place the ingredients inside.

Once sewn together, simply fill them with rice or flax seeds and lavender flowers. After that, all you will need to do is sew the opening left behind.

USAGE TIPS

To take full advantage of the relaxing effects of the pillow against headaches, you can store it in the refrigerator to obtain a cooling effect or, on the contrary, heat it a bit for a thermal effect. The pillow should be placed on the eyes while your head is resting or lying down. Keep it there for at least 25 minutes to get the relaxing benefits and ease the headache.

9 - BUTTER FOR INSECT STING

Bug bites are undeniably annoying. They can redden and create discomfort. The lightest scratching can also create abrasions on the skin.

Luckily, you can use an all-natural butter to soothe the itching and calm the redness.

This natural home remedy also helps heal and elasticize the skin, leaving a delicate scent in the air and on the skin that is both delicious and natural.

INGREDIENTS
- 10 drops of lavender essential oil
- 2 ½ tablespoons of beeswax
- 2 tablespoons of avocado oil
- 2 tablespoons of shea butter
- 5 drops of calendula oil
- 5 drops of tea tree oil

PREPARATION
To start, you will need a pot and a glass jar. The pot should be filled half to quarter full with water, while the beeswax, avocado oil, and shea butter should be placed in the glass jar. The jar will then be placed in the pot and the ingredients will melt in a bain-marie, which you should mix from time to time. After this, turn off the heat and add a few drops of various essential oils to the mixture.

Mixing while carefully amalgamate each ingredient with the other is the secret to obtaining an effective butter for insect bites.

Before it has completely cooled down, you can pour the mixture into smaller containers. Once done, you will have a butter capable of counteracting itching and redness to spread directly onto the sting without any concern.

USAGE TIPS
The natural composition helps soothe itching, moisturize the skin, and acts as an anti-inflammatory that eliminates swelling and redness while leaving a delicate scent on the skin. It is enough to last you for a long time and can be stored in a cool place, away from the sun.

10- OINTMENT

This ointment is a soothing ointment able to soften and moisturize the skin, and at the same time, treat anxiety and stress thanks to the freshness of calendula and lavender. This 100% natural method allows you to start in the right gear when daily commitments seem to get the better of our psychophysical balance and protect the skin from pollution. It is a powerful and healthy weapon that is easy to prepare.

INGREDIENTS
- 1 cup of dried calendula flowers
- 3 tablespoons of coconut oil
- ½ cup of dried lavender flowers
- 3 tablespoons of beeswax
- 15 drops of lavender essential oil
- 1 cup of extra virgin olive oil

PREPARATION
First, prepare a small glass jar to fill with the coconut oil and extra virgin olive oil, along with the dried lavender and calendula flowers. After, simply take a pot and fill it halfway up with water. Let the mixture in the jar simmer for 3 hours in a double boiler. When the mix is ready, it will be evident because an intense scent of flowers will spread all over the kitchen and the oil will change color. At this point, you must filter the mixture with a gauze or a tightly woven linen cloth to be wrung properly to let the oil come out. Once the oil has been collected in the jar, it will be possible to add the beeswax and cook over low heat until the wax has completely melted. Once the mixture is completely liquid, it will be possible to remove it from the heat and stir while adding lavender essential oil. Pour it into smaller containers before it solidifies.

USAGE TIPS
This relaxing ointment is excellent for relaxing muscles and moisturizing the skin, and can also soften the arch of the feet or decontract back massages. If well-stored and sealed when not used, this compound will last for a whole year.

LAVENDER ESSENTIAL OIL
35 Natural health remedies

CHAPPED LIPS: Add a dab of coconut oil to the palm. Mix one drop of lavender with a fingertip, then apply to the lips.

DANDRUFF: Add a few drops of lavender oil to your shampoo and massage onto the scalp to help eliminate dandruff. You can add tea tree oil, too. Doing this before bedtime may help you sleep better as well.

DRY SKIN: Combine a few drops of lavender essential oil with unscented lotion or carrier oil and apply to dry areas.

HAIR CARE: Add two drops to your hairbrush. Brush your hair. It will smell great and doing this helps to condition it naturally.

NAIL AND CUTICLE
TREATMENT: Warm up a small bowl of olive oil, add two drops of lavender, and stir. Dip your nails and cuticles into the mixture and soak for 5-10 minutes.

NATURAL BODY CLEANSER:

Instead of using soap when bathing or showering, apply three drops of lavender essential oil to a washcloth and scrub the entire body with it.

NATURAL DEODORANT:

First, eliminate any sweat present, then rub two drops of lavender essential oil under each arm. You may need to repeat this throughout the day, but it beats using chemical deodorants. Sweating is your body's natural way of expelling toxins, so it is essential to not use chemically toxic deodorants that block this process.

NATURAL DETANGLER: Add a few drops of lavender essential oil to your conditioner when in the shower. Apply to the hair, leave in for 1 min, and rinse out.

POST-WAXING/HAIR REMOVAL: Calm sensitive skin and soothe pores with a few drops of lavender in aloe vera gel. Apply to the affected area. Using lavender lotion is also helpful after shaving for men and women.

TIRED/SORE FEET: Fill a wide bowl with warm water. Add one teaspoon of jojoba oil mixed with four drops of lavender. Add 1/4 cup of Epsom salt for more relief. Soak feet for about 10 minutes. Apply lavender lotion after.

SCAR REDUCTION: To reduce the formation of scar tissue, massage rosehip oil and lavender essential oil on and around the affected area.

SHAVING NICKS: Use a tissue to dab a drop of lavender essential oil onto the nick.

SMELLY FEET: Add four drops of lavender essential oil to a bowl of warm water and mix. You can add Epsom salt for extra benefits. Soak feet for 5-10 minutes. Scrub with a cloth, pat dry, and apply lavender lotion.

STRETCH MARKS: Add a few drops of lavender essential oil to a carrier oil like rosehip seed oil and rub on the site. It's best to follow a daily application routine. Stretch marks will take time to fade but with persistence, they can do so.

WRINKLES/FACIAL SERUM: Add to facial moisturizer and apply to your face, especially to laugh lines and crows' feet (be sure to keep out of the eyes).

NATURAL CARPET FRESHENER: Mix 1/2 cup of baking soda with 10 drops of lavender essential oil and sprinkle on carpet. Wait 20 minutes and then vacuum up.

NOSEBLEEDS: Pinch the bridge of the nose and apply ice right above it. Apply one to two drops of lavender onto a tissue and place it under the nose.

POSTPARTUM: Beat the baby blues by inhaling lavender essential oil from an inhaler or by diffusing into the air.

PRETEST ANXIETY: Apply lavender roll onto your wrists before test time. If needed, during the test, deeply inhale the lavender aroma from your wrists. Another option is to use an infused tissue, apply a few drops to it, and keep it in your pocket. Using peppermint oil while studying and again during examinations has been clinically shown to improve grades up to 20%.

RASH/ITCHING: Apply to the location to stop the itch and support healing. Dilute in jojoba oil and apply to the desired area. Re-apply as needed.

RELIEVE STRESS: Diffuse lavender into the air or make a lavender room spray and spritz around you. Inhale deeply.

REPEL MOSQUITOES: Create a mosquito repellent lotion using one ounce of unscented lotion, nine drops of lavender, and three drops of lemongrass.

REPEL MOTHS AND INSECTS: Place a few drops of lavender essential oil on a cotton ball, then place them in linen closets or drawers to enhance the smell and repel bugs naturally. Try to add cedarwood essential oil, too.

RESPIRATORY RELIEF: Diffuse or use in a chest rub. Apply to nasal passages and the chest to help relieve coughs, seasonal allergies, and inflammation.

RINGWORM: Rub a few drops of lavender essential oil and coconut oil onto the affected area. Re-apply as needed. Be sure to wash your hands well after touching the spot to prevent spreading.

SINUS CONGESTION: Apply two drops to a bowl of hot water. Place a towel overhead, close your eyes, and breathe deeply for relief. This also helps soothe irritated nasal passages. Add one drop of eucalyptus essential oil to the water for additional comfort.

SORE MUSCLES: Combine three to six drops of lavender essential oil into one tablespoon of Castille soap or carrier oil (fractionated coconut oil or jojoba oil are best). Soak in the aromatherapy bath.

SORE THROATS: Add one drop of lavender essential oil to a warm glass of water. Stir well and gargle for 30 seconds, then spit out. Repeat two or three times per day.

SUNBURN RELIEF: Aloe vera gel and lavender form an excellent pair for sunburned skin. Keep your aloe vera gel in the refrigerator so that it is cold when you apply it. This makes it even more soothing. You may need to reapply frequently.

TEETH GRINDING: Before bedtime, apply a few drops of lavender to the jawbone up to the temples utilizing a roller bottle to help relax the jaw.

TENSION: Combine a few drops of lavender essential oil with a carrier oil for dilution and then massage into the neck, shoulder, and back.

VERTIGO/DIZZY SPELLS: Rub a few drops of lavender essential oil on the jawbone near the ear and the bone behind the ear.

DIY BEAUTY PRODUCTS

1- LAVENDER BODY OIL

Every day, our skin comes into contact with irritants, intense heat, cold, wind, smog, and more threatening elements. We owe it to ourselves to protect, moisturize, and take care of it. Giving it a scent of fresh flowers will relax acting in depth as an elasticizer, anti-stretch marks and strengthen our first defense barrier.

INGREDIENTS
- 2 teaspoons of dried lavender flowers, or alternatively, 4 teaspoons of fresh lavender flowers
- 6.7 ounces of cold-pressed sweet almond oil

PREPARATION
The preparation of this delicately scented oil is effortless. Start by pouring the almond oil into a glass jar. Then, take the dried or fresh lavender flowers and pound them in a mortar or in a bowl. Do not worry as the operation must not be too vigorous; it only serves to facilitate the release of the natural properties.

Afterward, you must put the flowers in the glass jar, while making sure to mix them well to cover them entirely with almond oil.

Once this operation has been accomplished, you may move on to the next step, which consists of closing the lid of the jar with gauze, linen cloth, or breathable fabric, and fix it with an elastic band or any other material.

The protected compound should be left to rest for 3-4 weeks, taking care of exposing it directly to the sun and protecting it from water. At the end of this period, it will be possible to filter the generated oil and keep it in a dark glass bottle to keep its properties intact.

With the glass or dark plastic dispenser dropper to protect the oil from light, you can apply the right amount along the eye area, face, and skin and massage gently to soothe muscle aches and pains, propagate a nice smell intensely, and fight anxiety and stress thanks to lavender, whose properties also have beneficial effects against free radicals and acts as a good moisturizer. In addition, this oil can be used for many other natural beauty recipes.

2- FACE SCRUB

Cleansing your face every now and then is not enough. A gentle scrub has emollient properties but helps eliminate impurities and hydrate the skin. At the same time, it reactivates the microcirculation that is essential for facial care with healthy and anti-aging effects. Moreover, this scrub that moisturizes and promotes the elimination of skin imperfections is a 100% natural beauty product.

INGREDIENTS
- 3 tablespoons of sea salt
- 1 tablespoon of organic liquid honey
- ¼ cup of sea salt
- ½ lemon
- 2 tablespoons of dried lavender
- 15 drops of lavender essential oil

PREPARATION
This facial scrub is gentle, highly aromatic, and elementary to prepare. A relatively large bowl will suffice. In this container, you will have to add all the ingredients, except the lavender essential oil drops, and mix them until you get a smooth mixture. Finally, add the 15 lavender drops and stir again.

USAGE TIPS
This preparation, used on damp skin, refreshes, regenerates, and purifies the skin, giving it greater elasticity and reactivating the microcirculation so as to eliminates wrinkles and imperfections. Leave it on for a few seconds while massaging gently before rinsing it with warm water.

3- LAVENDER AFTER SUN OIL

When exposed to the sun, the skin needs a proper after-sun oil that can defuse possible redness, soothe problems, and above all, moisturize thoroughly. Therefore, you could make your own scented after-sun, which contains all the characteristics described above, thanks to lavender. Moreover, in this case, taking care of your body will also mean taking care of the environment because the 100% natural ingredients will not be polluting once dissolved in water.

INGREDIENTS
- 6 teaspoons of argan oil
- 5 drops of roman chamomile essential oil
- 6 teaspoons of coconut oil
- 5 drops of geranium essential oil
- 10 drops of lavender essential oil

PREPARATION
Pour 6 teaspoons of coconut oil into a glass container to be placed in the microwave. Leave it for a few minutes, until it is completely liquefied. Then, let it cool, and add 6 teaspoons of argan oil before adding the drops of essential oils. Decant into smaller and easily transportable containers.

USAGE TIPS
Use on damp skin after showering after a day at the beach. Cover every part of the body with a small layer and let it absorb the mixture. With this product, you will have utterly hydrated skin while benefiting from soothing and anti-inflammatory properties. Complete absorption is recommended before exposure to the sun.

4- LIQUID HAND SOAP

There are some things which, once you know how to prepare, can no longer do without. Among them, liquid hand soap is an indispensable pleasure. It is an excellent disinfectant that protects the skin and gives it an intense aroma of lavender that will not go unnoticed. The recipe is simple and allows you to save on the purchase of countless hand soaps.

INGREDIENTS
- ¾ cup of castile soap
- ¾ cup of distilled water
- 1 tablespoon of vitamin E oil
- 1 tablespoon of sweet almond or jojoba oil
- 10-15 drops of melaleuca essential oil
- 5-10 drops of lavender essential oil
- 1 tablespoon of glycerin
- 16-ounce glass jar
- Cap with dispensing pump

PREPARATION

In a glass jar, first add the water to avoid the formation of bubbles. Then, pour the liquid castile soap, and finally, the oils and glycerin. The recipe does not require cooking. Instead, simply shake the ingredients well and keep the jar near the sink.

USAGE TIPS

The foaming pump will make the product last much longer. Before washing your hands, you will need to shake the bottle a bit, and then, dispense this fabulous, scented foam on your hands. The ingredients in this recipe are natural and beneficial to the skin, so you can also use this liquid soap for the body to nourish, moisturize, and leave a scent on your skin.

5- BODY SCRUB

Scrubs are an essential step for deep cleansing the skin and allowing cell renewal. Natural scrubs are also beneficial to improve the skin's appearance and act on circulation through small massaging movements that can be done in the shower. However, a body scrub is different from a face scrub, which needs to be more delicate. This lavender body scrub is designed to leave your skin silky smooth and fragrant.

INGREDIENTS
- 1 cup of raw sugar
- 3 drops of lavender essential oil (or more if you want a stronger scent)

- 4-5 tablespoons of organic coconut oil
- 1 tablespoon of fresh lavender petals

PREPARATION

Coconut oil can be hard when cold, so you need to microwave it for 10-20 seconds for it to return to its liquid state. Next, pour raw sugar soaked with essential oil of lavender in a large bowl, and finally, add coconut oil. Stir with a wooden spoon and place everything in a jar with a large opening or airtight container. Use the lavender flowers to make your scrub beautiful and even more fragrant and relaxing in the shower.

USAGE TIPS

This is a powerful exfoliant because of the size of the sugar grains, which is why you can use it a couple of times a week on specific body parts, such as rough feet, elbows, or knees by rubbing in gentle circular motions to increase circulation in the desired areas. Lavender is highly healing and suitable for acne breakouts, for example, while coconut oil is very nourishing. Thus, once you've gone through the body scrub, you don't need to use any other creams. The sugar might melt a bit but you can replace it with salt.

6 - NOURISHING BATH SALTS

The scents given off by lavender have exceptional power in relaxing the body and mind, relieving muscle aches after a long day, and balancing the mind by providing peace and well-being. Of course, there is nothing better than a warm bath to let the fresh, natural notes do the work. A moment of healthy relaxation is all you need sometimes, and you should be able to treat yourself with class.

INGREDIENTS

- 2 cups of dead sea salt
- 10 drops of lavender essential oil
- 1 tablespoon of coconut oil
- 2 cups of Epsom salt
- ½ cup of dried lavender sprouts
- ½ cup of dried chamomile shoots

PREPARATION

First, you need to place the salts and dried sprouts inside a bowl and mix until the mixture is well blended. In a separate cup, mix coconut oil and lavender essential oil, making sure the mixture is uniform. Afterward, you can combine the ingredients, collect them in a linen cloth or muslin bag to immediately obtain an incredible bath salt, ready to release a fabulous aroma and relaxing and decontracting properties that will make a hot bath feel like a real aromatherapy experience.

USAGE TIPS

Leave the sachet to soak for 10-20 minutes, and then, remove it.
What remains inside can be stored in a jar in a dry, light-free environment for up to 6 months for reuse. This bath has moisturizing and softening properties on the skin, which will feel immediately relaxed.

7- BODY LOTION

This homemade lavender oil body lotion is perfect after a stressful day at work and a rejuvenating shower. Besides, it's also an all-natural lotion suitable for aiding your baby's sleep.

INGREDIENTS
- 1 cup of aloe vera gel
- 2 tablespoons of vegetable-based emulsifying wax
- ½ cup of almond oil
- 1 tablespoon of shea butter
- 15-20 drops of lavender essential oil
- 1 teaspoon of vanilla extract

PREPARATION

Unite the wax, shea butter, and almond oil in a small saucepan and stir together until melted. At this point, you can let the mixture cool without letting it harden completely. Next, in a separate bowl, mix the aloe vera gel, vanilla, and lavender essential oil. Add the resulting mixture to the softened wax, and with a blender, start whipping. The recipe can also be made without wax. In this case, you will need half a cup of coconut oil, half a cup of sweet almond oil, and one cup of shea butter and of lavender drops. The essential step is to whip the butter so that it becomes creamy.

USAGE TIPS
The resulting lotion will be very frothy and highly moisturizing, suitable for the winter months, when the skin needs external help to regain its vigor. The cream can be stored in glass jars with convenient and practical lids. Coconut oil contains natural fatty acids that protect, heal, and soothe the skin. Meanwhile, shea butter is a superfood for the skin because it is naturally rich in vitamins A, E, and F. The regular use of this body butter will provide your skin with a burst of nourishment that will keep you glowing all day long.

8- EYE MAKEUP REMOVER

The eyes are a particularly sensitive part of the face that should only be treated with natural ingredients and all the necessary care. In addition, the removal of makeup residues is essential, and sometimes, a simple makeup remover wipe is not enough to get rid of everything and is too aggressive. For this reason, you can prepare an eye makeup remover with your own hands and natural ingredients.

INGREDIENTS
- ½ cup of coconut oil
- 10 drops of lavender essential oil
- Small resealable glass jar

PREPARATION
Although the ingredients are few, they are highly effective and natural. Coconut oil may not come in a liquid form, so you can dissolve it in the microwave or heat it in a saucepan until it becomes liquid. At this point, just pour it into the glass jar, add lavender oil, and mix with a spoon until you get a homogeneous mixture. Store it in a cool place away from light.

USAGE TIPS
Instead of using cotton pads, you can use reusable cloth pads. Just wrap one around your finger, dip it in the oil, and gently remove makeup from your eyes. Coconut oil provides highly moisturizing effects, and therefore, does not dry out the eyes.

9- LAVENDER TONIC

A toner is an essential product within the daily routine because it brightens the face by tightening the pores and making the skin appear immediately relaxed and soothed. This chamomile and lavender toner is especially perfect for sensitive skin because it is soothing and best dabbed in the evening, at the end of a stressful day.

INGREDIENTS
- 3 ½ ounces of chamomile infusion
- ¼ of a teaspoon of vegetable glycerin
- 1/8 of a teaspoon of xanthan gum
- 8 drops of lavender essential oil
- 18 drops of organic Cosgard preservatives

PREPARATION
Prepare the chamomile infusion with water and infused chamomile sachets or flowers. While the chamomile is infusing, add the glycerin and xanthan gum in a glass container and begin mixing. Little by little, add the infusion of chamomile to avoid the formation of lumps and forming a sort of gel. Slowly add the drops of lavender essential oil and of preservatives. Then, using a filter, you can put the gel inside a container with a pump cap.

USAGE TIPS
Use the poured toner on a cotton pad by dabbing it gently on the skin. Chamomile is very gentle, and lavender is also particularly good for sensitive skin. Preserving the product will ensure that the toner lasts for at least 4 months. Before using the toner, shake it a bit to prevent the oils inside from dispersing.

10- LAVENDER HAND CREAM

Frequent washings inevitably worsen the state of the skin of your hands. Dry skin, cracks, cuts, cuticles, and peels are neither aesthetically pleasing nor pleasant to the touch. For this reason, a good hand cream must meet several requirements, because, in addition to deeply moisturizing the skin, it must be well-scented, sanitizing, natural, and nourishing. This recipe for hand cream leaves a little greasy texture on the hands but provides stunning results.

INGREDIENTS
- ⅓ cup of sweet almond oil
- 2 tablespoons of coconut oil
- 2 tablespoons of olive oil
- 3 tablespoons of grated beeswax
- 35 drops of lavender essential oil

PREPARATION

Combine the oils in a saucepan and heat over medium heat. These will need to be barely warm. Then, let stand for 5 minutes. Once removed from the heat, simply add the grated beeswax, stirring it until it is completely melted. Add the essential oil and refrigerate for 10 minutes.

At this point, the cream can be poured into a container and left to cool completely.

USAGE TIPS

The cream can be stored in a cool, dry place and will have a harder consistency in the winter. This cream does not absorb easily and remains a bit greasy on the hands but has a potent effect on hydration, appearance, and skin improvement in the long run. That's why you can make overnight compresses to apply with gloves on. If you dilute it even more, you can put it in a jar with a pump lid and make it easier to carry.

11 - LAVENDER LIP BUTTER

Lips are prone to all kinds of problems because they get exposed to cold or sun and are sensitive. Lip balm is a faithful companion for anyone; some even carry more than one at all times. This recipe is easy to make and will keep your lips moisturized, soft, and protected.

INGREDIENTS
- 2 ounces of organic crushed or grated beeswax
- 3 ounces of organic coconut oil
- 5 drops of vitamin E
- 10 drops of therapeutic lavender essential oil

PREPARATION

Place the beeswax and coconut oil in a water bath to melt over medium heat, stirring occasionally to make the mixture very smooth. At this point, you can add the vitamins E and therapeutic lavender essential oil. Carefully pour into a metal lip balm container as the mixture will be very hot. Allow it to cool.

USAGE TIPS

The balm can be used once the mixture has cooled down. Lavender and coconut oil are gentle and pleasant to use on lips, which will be left naturally moisturized and soft.

12 - LAVENDER NOURISHING HAIR MASK

We all have to deal with dry and damaged hair, whether due to natural agents like wind or sun or because of shampoos and chemicals used on our hair. For this reason, it is vital to use a natural and healing product that is highly nourishing.
On the hair, lavender has a deeply moisturizing and detangling effect and gives an intense scent that hardly goes unnoticed.

INGREDIENTS

- 3 tablespoons of coconut oil
- 1 tablespoon of olive oil
- 8 drops of lavender essential oil

PREPARATION

The ingredients should be placed all together in a clean container and whipped with a blender until you get a thick and creamy mixture. This mixture will be highly moisturizing and nourishing for the hair, and for this reason, should be rinsed out.

USAGE TIPS

The cream obtained can be applied to dry and clean hair and combed through to distribute it better. Leave it on for 15-20 minutes. Then, rinse, shampoo, and dry your hair as usual. Repeat the operation as often as desired. Keep the cream inside an airtight container in a dry, shady place.

13 - SHAVING CREAM

Shaving cream is not a cosmetic reserved for men: when you shave your beard or cut the hair on your legs, the layer of new skin that is created is very delicate and at risk of redness. That is why it is not recommended to use ready-made products that contain harmful ingredients to the skin. Instead, this cream includes soothing, scented lavender for a soothing effect.

INGREDIENTS
- 1 airtight container
- 2 tablespoons of sweet almond oil
- ¼ cup of coconut oil
- ¼ cup of shea butter
- 4 drops of lavender essential oil
- 2 drops of eucalyptus essential oil

PREPARATION
In a water bath, melt coconut oil and shea butter, add sweet almond oil when they are completely melted, and whisk. Then, leave it to rest in the fridge. The cooled mixture will have a buttery smooth appearance. After, you can add drops of refreshing eucalyptus oil and calming lavender oil and continue whipping. This recipe has a total yield of 8 ounces, and you can store the shaving cream in an airtight container.

USAGE TIPS
If you use this shaving cream in the shower, be careful not to slip. It's always best to use a non-slip mat when dealing with such oily products. To shave, you must have a shaving brush and proceed as follows:

1. Wet the brush in lukewarm water.
2. Dip it into the shaving cream.
3. Apply shaving cream to damp skin in a thin layer.
4. Starting from the ankle, shave up to the knee.
5. Rinse the blade and repeat.

14 - MAKEUP BRUSH CLEANER

Makeup brushes are often used without considering that they can be harmful to the health of the skin. Indeed, they attract and retain many bacteria that cause problems for those with acne-prone or sensitive skin.

Makeup is applied practically every day, but brushes are not washed as often as they should be to maintain perfect skin.

INGREDIENTS
- 4-ounce dispenser bottle
- 4 ounces of liquid castile soap
- 3 drops of melaleuca essential oil
- 3 drops of lavender essential oil

PREPARATION

Castile soap is very effective against bacteria that settle inside makeup brushes. To prepare a perfect cleanser for makeup brushes, pour the liquid soap inside the bottle with drops of melaleuca essential oil, which has anti-fungal and antibacterial properties against streptococci and fungi, as well as lavender essential oil, which is antiseptic.

USAGE TIPS
1. Dampen the bristles of the brush.
2. Squeeze a small amount of the cleanser onto the bristles.
3. Lather the bristles in a circular motion against the palm of your hand.
4. Rinse without involving the handle.
5. Shake and reshape the bristles by laying the brush on a dry cloth overnight.

If you wear makeup five or more days a week, you should clean your brushes once a week.

LAVENDER ESSENTIAL OIL: 15 Natural Beauty Remedies

1. CHAPPED LIPS

Add a dab of coconut oil to the palm, mix one drop of lavender in with a fingertip, and then apply to the lips.

Add a few drops of lavender oil to your shampoo and massage onto the scalp to help eliminate dandruff. You can add tea tree oil too. Making this before bedtime may help you sleep better as well.

2. DANDRUFF

3. DRY SKIN

Combine a few drops of lavender essential oil with unscented lotion or carrier oil and apply to dry areas.

Add two drops to your hairbrush. Brush your hair. It will smell great, and doing this helps to condition it naturally.

4. HAIR CARE

5. NAIL and CUTICLE TREATMENT

Warm up a small bowl of olive oil, add in 2 drops of lavender, and stir. Dip nails and cuticles into the mixture, soak for 5-10 minutes.

Instead of using soap when bathing or showering, apply three drops of lavender essential oil to a washcloth and scrub the entire body.

6. NATURAL BODY CLEANSER

7. NATURAL DEODORANT

Eliminate any sweat present first, and then rub two drops of lavender essential oil under each arm. It May need to be repeated during the day, but it beats using chemical deodorants.

Add a few drops of lavender essential oil to conditioner when in the shower, apply to the hair, leave in for 1 minute and then rinse out.

8. NATURAL DETANGLER

9. POST WAXING/HAIR REMOVAL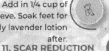

Calm sensitive skin and soothe pores with a few drops of lavender in aloe vera gel. Apply to the affected area. Using lavender lotion is also helpful after shaving for men and women.

Fill a wide bowl with warm water. Add one teaspoon of jojoba oil mixed with four drops of lavender. Add in 1/4 cup of Epsom salt for more relieve. Soak feet for about 10 minutes. Apply lavender lotion after.

10. TIRED/SORE FEET

11. SCAR REDUCTION

To reduce scar tissue formation, massage rosehip oil and lavender essential oil on and around the affected area.

Dab a drop of lavender essential oil onto nick with an issue.

12. SHAVING NICKS

Add four drops of lavender essential oil to a warm bowl of water and mix around. You can add Epsom salt for more extra benefits. Soak feet for 5-10 minutes, next scrub with cloth, pat dry and apply lavender lotion. Fresh again.

13. SMELLY FEET

Add a few drops of lavender essential oil to carrier oil like rosehip seed oil and rub on location. Best to have a daily application routine. Stretch marks will take time to fade. But, with persistence, they can fade.

14. STRETCH MARKS

15. WRINKLES/FACIAL SERUM

Add to facial moisturizer & apply to face, especially to laugh lines and crows feet (careful to keep out of eyes).

HANDMADE GIFTS

1 - NATURAL SOAP WITH SHEA BUTTER AND LAVENDER

When it comes to giving a gift to a loved one, it is crucial to surprise, and at the same time, give them something with a high emotional value and made from the heart. A handmade gift is undoubtedly much more valuable than a purchased one.

Besides, you can customize it at will to respect the character of the person you are gifting it to.

This soap is easy to make and natural.

INGREDIENTS
- 10.5 ounces of olive oil
- 2.6 ounces of sweet almond oil
- 3.5 ounces of shea butter
- 6 teaspoons of castor oil
- 5.3 ounces of distilled water
- 2.2 ounces of caustic soda
- 25 drops of lavender essential oil
- As many dried lavender buds as desired
- Molds to taste

PREPARATION
Wearing gloves and goggles, pour all the oils into a saucepan, along with shea butter. Place on the stove and heat until the butter melts while stirring. In a separate container, prepare caustic soda and water. Then, pour the soda into the water (and not the other way around) and carefully stir with a metal spoon.

As soon as the oil and butter are ready, the mixture can be removed from the heat. When the oil and soda reach a temperature between 95 and 105°F, mix the two preparations, stir and blend everything. Then, whisk with an immersion blender to obtain a creamy consistency, and add the lavender drops. Keep mixing and pour the mixture into the chosen molds, preferably made of silicone to make the soap bar easier to remove. The mixture can provide you with 6 bars of soap of about 2.8 oz. each. Once the mixture has been poured into the molds, cover the soaps with plastic wrap, and then, with a cotton cloth. Let rest outside the refrigerator for 36 to 48 hours, until completely solidified.

USAGE TIPS
Before using it, the soap should be allowed to cure for 40 days in a dry place. Then, you can apply lavender pods as desired, either in the mixture or in the mold. This soap is perfect for the face and body as it has velvety and emollient properties. Meanwhile, the lavender smell leaves your skin smelling great and relaxes you in the shower. In addition, you can wrap these bars of soap in decorative paper and ribbons by inserting decorative and scented lavender sprigs.

2 - LAVENDER RAG DOLL

Rag dolls and soft toys are always lovely gifts. They can represent anything from animals to beautiful girls with blonde braids. In this case, in addition to decorating the environment, this doll will be relaxing to hold and highly fragrant. A real gift with flakes!

INGREDIENTS
- 10.5 ounces of dried lavender buds
- One small rag doll
- 2 drops of lavender essential oil
- Needles and thread

PREPARATION
Take a small rag doll, make a hole at the base of the back, and pull out the stuffing. Fill the doll with dried lavender buds, and stitch the hole with needles and thread. Add 2 drops of lavender essential oil to the fabric.

USAGE TIPS

When choosing the doll, you can think of a curious little animal, like an owl or lizard, or consider the tastes of the person who will receive the gift. Thanks to the dried lavender buds, holding this gift in your hand will be like having a stress reliever, and the calming properties of lavender will invade the room, spreading the smell from this beautiful gift.

3 - LAVENDER BATH BOMB

What could be more relaxing than a nice bath filled with the scent of calming, stress-relieving lavender at the end of the day? Bath bombs are a little luxury to indulge in from time to time, and thanks to the essential oil of lavender, you can get a relaxing bath. Plus, with lavender bath bombs, you can give this emotion to the people you love the most.

INGREDIENTS

- 1 cup of baking soda
- 1 cup of citric acid
- ½ cup of cornstarch
- ½ cup of coconut oil
- 8 drops of purple food coloring
- 8 drops of lavender essential oil
- Dried lavender buds for decoration
- Stencils

PREPARATION

First, you need to combine all the dry ingredients and mix them well. Then, add purple food coloring and the therapeutic grade lavender essential oil. At this point, you just need to heat the coconut oil to make it liquid and add it to the dry mix. Then, mix with your hands. You will obtain a sort of moist, colorful sand that you must press into the chosen molds, previously filled with a few decorative lavender buds. Allow it to dry for about 12 hours, and then, gently remove each bomb from its mold.

To use the bath bombs, simply place them at the bottom of the bathtub while bathing. In addition, the bombs can be placed in a hand-decorated bag to be donated on any occasion.

4 - NATURAL LAVENDER PERFUME

Making a DIY perfume is convenient, eliminates chemicals, and helps implement a more natural daily routine. If you suffer from sensitive skin, it is the ideal heartfelt gift. In addition, lavender has calming properties and helps with blood circulation. With this recipe, making perfume at home is quick and easy.

INGREDIENTS
- Small jar with ball roll to store the perfume
- 10 drops of lavender essential oil
- 10 drops of vanilla essential oil
- Fractionated coconut oil or sweet almond oil
- Optional: fresh flower buds

PREPARATION
You can prepare a homemade perfume with these few simple steps. First, add 10 drops of vanilla essential oil and 10 drops of lavender essential oil to the bottle.
These will create the perfect scent and a sweet, relaxing mix.
The rest of the bottle should be filled with fractioned coconut oil. It will be enough to insert the cap with the ball and shake the ingredients well. Some fresh flowers inside the bottle will make everything more delicate and refined. The important thing is to insert them before the coconut oil.

USAGE TIPS
Enjoy it! Gift this wonderful lavender and vanilla perfume to anyone you want, as it is completely natural and free of chemical additives. You can apply the perfume as desired on the wrists, the base of the neck, or on the body. No matter where you spray it, coconut oil always has a moisturizing effect.

5 - SUGAR SCRUB SOAP

Scrubbing is an essential step in everyone's beauty routine because it helps remove imperfections from the skin and make it smoother and brighter. These sugar scrub soaps with lavender essential oil are very easy to make at home and are an exceptional gift for friends and family members, who will be left speechless.

INGREDIENTS
- Silicone molds of any shape
- ¼ cup of coconut oil
- ½ cup of melted soap
- 1 cup of sugar
- Colorant
- 15-20 drops of lavender essential oil

PREPARATION
First, melt the soap in a Pyrex glass cup for 15 seconds in the microwave. Once you have melted soap, mix it with coconut oil and sugar while stirring. Add a few drops of food coloring to taste. The mixture is then grainy, but if it hardens too much, you can put it back in the microwave. Afterward, pour the mixture into silicone molds.

USAGE TIPS
To get a moisturizing scrub, you can add some shea butter or vegetable glycerin. The mixture should be left to rest for two hours. The resulting bars can be used in the shower and have a moisturizing, cleansing, and calming effect thanks to lavender.

6 - LAVENDER MOISTURIZING LOTION

Another product for cosmetics that can be deemed indispensable is moisturizing lotion. These lotions look like bars and allow you to maintain hydrated skin. You can take them everywhere, even on the plane, and they are a perfect gift for those who suffer from dry skin or chapped hands during the winter. Convenient, practical, and fragrant, these lavender moisturizing bars are effortless to prepare.

INGREDIENTS
- 1 cup of organic extra virgin coconut oil
- ¼ cup of shea butter
- ¼ cup of 100% organic beeswax
- Lavender essential oil
- ¼ tablespoon of vitamin E
- Silicone molds

PREPARATION

Coconut oil should be carefully melted together with shea butter and beeswax until the mixture reaches a completely liquid form. Then, you can put the ingredients together and let them melt in a water bath. The beeswax melts faster and easier when grated. Once the wax and oils are melted, you can add the vitamin E, after which you need to let the mixture cool a bit before adding about 15-20 drops of lavender. Once it is all blended, pour the product into silicone molds and let it harden. You can also add color to taste before pouring it into the molds.

USAGE TIPS

These lotion bars are intensely moisturizing, and their properties come out simply when in contact with the heat of the skin. It is a simple to prepare, homemade recipe, and beautiful gift. You can easily carry them inside your handbag and take them with you on the coldest days.

7 - GREETING CARD WITH PAPER SEEDS

Sometimes, making a gift seems impossible because there is so much choice, so many alternatives, and so little time; and a greeting card is not enough. Or at least, not an ordinary greeting card. This one is made entirely by hand and contains seeds, which means it can be put in a pot and will grow into a beautiful plant. This is the only way to make a greeting card the actual gift.

INGREDIENTS
- 8-10 sheets of shredded paper
- 1 packet of seeds to taste
- 1 heaped tablespoon of dried lavender or other flowers and leaves
- Cookie shapes

- Tools
- Colander
- Blender
- Towel
- Cardboard
- Printer
- Scissors and glue

PREPARATION

Shred pieces of paper, whether they are old pieces, scrap paper, or any other type of paper without a glossy finish. If you want to get colored paper, just add a piece and shred it. Place the paper in boiling water for 45 minutes to an hour to make it soft and easy to break down. Pour the paper into a blender until it is half full, and pour in about a cup of the water it was soaked in. Blend a few times until you obtain a pasty pulp. If necessary, add more water to achieve this consistency. Pour the resulting pulp through a strainer into a bowl to remove some of the moisture. At this point, mix the seeds into the still moist paper pulp. Choose seeds that can be planted together.

Lay cotton towels on a flat surface, spread out, and let the paper dry for a day or more. Then, spread the pulp and pat it dry. You may also use a rolling pin to roll out the pulp. Either way, the important thing is to be careful not to break the seeds. Once dry, you can cut out shapes as desired and write cute messages.

USAGE TIPS

Remember to include instructions on the card, such as, "The paper on this card is made of plantable seeds." Before planting, tear it into many small pieces, put them in a pot, and cover it with a finger of soil.

8 - LAVENDER SPRAY BEARD DETANGLER

Long beards are all the rage, and many men are very careful to keep them healthy, thick, and well-combed. Thus, a 100% natural and handmade beard detangler is a great gift. It's a simple way to tell someone that you've been thinking about them and that you know how important it is for them to look well-groomed.

INGREDIENTS
- 4 teabags of organic green tea
- 4 teaspoons of aloe gel
- 8 drops of lavender essential oil
- 6 ¼ cup of pharmaceutical ampoule

PREPARATION
Let the 4 green tea bags steep in a cup of boiling water for 15-20 minutes. Then, add aloe gel and 8 drops of lavender essential oil. Decant into a medical ampoule.

USAGE TIPS
The medical ampoule is a small bottle with a really elegant cork that you can find inside herbalist shops and that keeps, with its darkened glass, the properties of the detangler. To use it, you only need to spray it onto the beard and gently massage the product with your fingers, making sure to distribute it evenly from the tip of the beard to the root. This product offers many benefits. For sentence, green tea is an antioxidant that protects against the elements and smog. Meanwhile, aloe oil takes care of the hair, making it more disciplined. Finally, lavender provides antibacterial and scenting action.

HOME DÉCOR

HOW TO DRY LAVENDER

Lavender is a beautiful flower to behold, with a color that is nothing short of unique and inimitable. There is no flower more fragrant nor more suitable for home decorations than lavender. It is also a multifaceted flower which, once dried, can be used in various ways. Besides, its virtues are countless.

TOOLS
- Lavender flowers
- Twine

PREPARATION
The optimal period for harvesting lavender is between July and August. The secret to obtaining a perfect result from a chromatic point of view is to pick the stems loaded with flowers still in bud, just before they open. To dry lavender, all you need to do is gather it in bunches and hang it upside down

in a shaded but well-ventilated area. The sun will tend to discolor the vivid color of lavender. Next, lavender sprigs will need to be pruned to a length of 8 inches and you will have to keep the spikes tightly packed. Finally, the flowers can be ginned up with your fingers or a comb, dropping the flowers on a cotton cloth.

USAGE TIPS
Collected buds are perfect for scented bags and flavored potpourri, while dried lavender flowers can be used to make garlands and many other decorations for the interior, giving a rustic style to a home.

1 - GARLAND

Who said that garlands are only made at Christmas? Braiding flowers is a very relaxing practice that provides aesthetically pleasing results, even in the summer. To make this summer garland, you only need a few ingredients. With those, not only will you have a gorgeous and decorative item for your home, but you will be flooded with the fresh scent of lavender.

TOOLS
- Handcrafted floral ring
- Twine
- Scissors
- Lavender flowers

PREPARATION
For an 18-inch diameter ring, you will need to call on 3-4 lavender plants. For a 12" one, you might only need 2-3. Either way, the stems will need to be at least 12-15 inches long.
At this point, you will only need to start pinning the lavender flowers to the ring with twine. Ideally, you want to group 12 flowers at a time and secure them to the ring.
Proceed like this and fill in the empty spots as you go until the circle is complete.

A tip is to group as many flowers as possible around this wreath because, over time, they will tend to dry and shrink. Then, hang the wreath at the door to welcome visitors, or if you made smaller versions, inside the house.
They will be particularly valuable for their fragrance.

2 - VINTAGE PAINTING WITH LAVENDER

Lavender is a very unique flower that lends itself to multi-faceted uses. A lavender flower has an intense color, a fragrant smell, and a special appearance. No flower has a shape so harmonious and that lends itself to many types of ideas and handmade creations.
Lavender is a true work of art that will transform your rooms, creating a country atmosphere.

TOOLS
- Old painting with frame
- 1 sheet of white scrapbook paper
- Spray adhesive
- Dried lavender
- A couple of heavy books

PREPARATION
First, pull out the painting from the frame and apply the sheet of white scrapbook paper using adhesive. Then, choose some lavender stems, lay them on a paper towel, and press them with heavy books overnight. To attach the lavender stems to the canvas, cover the surface with more spray adhesive and position them as desired.
Next, spray some adhesive over the lavender to help it stick. At this point, simply reinsert the canvas into the frame and hang it up.

USAGE TIPS
The chosen frame creates a nice contrast to the lavender flowers. You can use any type of old frame that is no longer used. In this way, you can create entire sets to reproduce the same concept in different rooms of your house.

3 - CENTERPIECE WITH LAVENDER

A beautiful table setting cannot do without striking, brightly-colored centerpieces with an intense — yet not annoying — aroma.

Centerpieces bring about a touch of style, even on the living room or kitchen tables when you are not holding large lunches or dinners but simply want to gather around something cozy.

Lavender lends itself perfectly to these decorations because it stimulates table conversation and calmness in the participants.

TOOLS

- Metal or wicker basket
- Burlap sack
- Fresh lavender flowers

PREPARATION

To make a centerpiece with a rustic style and a Provencal touch, you should use tools found in many homes and customize as desired. The idea is that the centerpiece remains simple, with a burlap inside the basket and beautiful lavender flowers inside, or directly the flowerpot.

USAGE TIPS

Lay the lavender centerpiece on top of a rough canvas runner. Lavender is a flower that does not go unnoticed. For this reason, it does not need to surround itself with garish colors. Besides, in order not to make it look too full, it is better to use softer shades for the rest of the decor.

4 - LAVENDER SUMMER BASKET

Lavender has a Provençal style that can also enrich the outdoors, such as garden tables, the entrance, or the back patio. A lavender summer basket is easily made in less than 10 minutes and can be used both outside and inside. For example, it is perfect for a picnic photoshoot or to keep in the cottage.

TOOLS

- Wicker basket with a handle
- Lavender
- Faux dill bushes

- Plastic bags or crumpled sheets of paper for volume
- Canvas or jute bag
- Wreath ring the same size as the basket

PREPARATION

Place the plastic bags or crumpled paper at the base of the wicker basket to give the dill and lavender a base to stand on. Then, use jute or canvas to cover the plastic. Next, make a garland with the lavender and place it on the edge of the basket. Finally, in the center, place the dill with a few lavender stems.

USAGE TIPS

This quick and easy summer lavender basket can be used in the entryway, as part of a simple table centerpiece, or for a summer-inspired vignette. One tip is not to set out to buy tools but to make something with what you already have around the house.

5 - LAVENDER ROOM DIFFUSERS

Room diffusers are also very much in vogue thanks to their aesthetic. They can be placed anywhere and leave a soft and delicate smell when you are in their vicinity. Unsurprisingly, they are perfect for offices and other rooms that require concentration, such as studies and entryways, where lavender will make you feel even more at home as soon as you enter the house.

TOOLS
- Glass or ceramic container
- 70% sweet almond oil
- 20% lavender essential oil
- 10% orange essential oil
- Bamboo sticks

PREPARATION

Pour in the almond and essential oils and mix. The almond oil allows the essential oils to decrease their viscosity and release the aroma. The top note is definitely the lavender oil, which, combined with orange oil, creates a very intense atmosphere.

USAGE TIPS

Leave the sticks to soak for an hour before turning them over. Then, turn them over again after a week. Due to the high percentage of essential oils, this recipe is perfect for small yet super scented diffusers. The diffusers for small rooms act as decor.

NATURAL HOUSE CLEANING PRODUCTS

1 - ANTIBACTERIAL LAVENDER CARPET AND RUG CLEANER

Inside carpets and rugs are more likely to create favorable conditions for the proliferation of bacteria and parasites harmful to the whole family's health. Eliminating this problem and removing all traces of bacteria without using chemicals is possible thanks to the properties of lavender and a 100% natural detergent.

INGREDIENTS
- 5 drops of lavender essential oil
- 1 cup of baking soda
- 1 salt shaker

PREPARATION
Take a bowl and fill it with 1 cup of baking soda. Next, add lavender essential oil and stir until fully absorbed. Then, take a salt shaker and fill it with the product you've just made.

USAGE TIPS
Use the salt shaker to dispense this bactericidal and anti-mite powder and spread the product on the dirty carpets and rugs. Allow 20 minutes for baking soda's combined action, which will absorb dirt and odors, and for lavender, which will scent the environment and eliminate bacteria. Then, remove traces with a vacuum cleaner or hard-bristled floor brush.

2 - CREAMY LAVENDER CLEANER

Cleaning your home is an important task and doing it in a completely eco-friendly way is our duty to the planet. However, perhaps not everyone knows that making a detergent at home is very easy and inexpensive.

Plus, you tend to save money in the long run as you can make detergents that last a long time.

INGREDIENTS
- Baking soda
- Eco-friendly dish soap
- Organic lavender essential oil
- Glass jar with cap
- Wooden spoon

PREPARATION
Fill the glass jar with baking soda. Then, slowly pour eco-friendly dish soap and mix until you obtain a kind of cream. Next, add 10 drops of organic lavender essential oil.

USAGE TIPS
It has good degreasing power on the sink and stove, bathroom fixtures, and after cleaning and degreasing, makes all surfaces shine. It is a non-toxic and non-harmful product that has the properties, thanks to lavender, to relax you and remove tensions while you are doing housework.

3 - WOOD POLISH

Cleaning wood has always been an affair that requires commitment, unique products, and is super expensive. Still, you can get the same results by hand making an all-natural product that is not harmful to the environment.

In addition, these products are inexpensive and very easy to use, allowing you to save in the long run as you can choose the amount of product to make and put the rest aside for the next cleaning.

INGREDIENTS
- Organic beeswax
- Extra virgin olive oil
- Lavender essential oil
- Glass jar

PREPARATION

Pour an equal amount of beeswax and olive oil and heat the ingredients while stirring. As soon as done, remove from heat and allow to cool. As soon as it starts to cool, add the lavender drops and pour the mixture into a jar.

USAGE TIPS

This preparation can be used from the next day.

It is a very delicate, and at the same time, intense polish that makes the wood shine. In addition, lavender will provide both antibacterial effects and a deep and intense aroma.

4 - NATURAL CLEANER FOR ALL SURFACES

To do general house cleaning, it is often necessary to use a detergent that is effective yet not aggressive, and suitable for all surfaces.

This recipe calls for one that is all-natural and handmade at home with everyday ingredients and a nice handful of dried lavender flowers, which clean, scent and sanitize the surfaces.

INGREDIENTS
- 1 cup of vinegar
- ¼ cup of dried lavender
- Water
- Spray cleaner bottle
- Filter

PREPARATION

In a glass jar, mix the vinegar and dried lavender, then seal it. Let the mixture sit in a sunny place for 10 days. Once that time has elapsed, filter the lavender and keep the infused vinegar that can be mixed with water in this way: 1-part infused vinegar and 2 parts water.

USAGE TIPS

Use this vinegar cleaner as you would any all-purpose cleaner, i.e., spray and wipe. It is a good cleaner for tables, glass, mirrors, refrigerators, bathrooms, children's toys, in other words, anywhere. The only thing you need to be careful of is granite and marble because vinegar tends to degrade these surfaces.

5 - REFRESHING ROOM SPRAY

A good scent is often synonymous with cleanliness. For this reason, walking into a place and smelling the fresh scent of lavender will be like walking into a freshly disinfected and cleaned environment. This room freshener is perfect to spray right after airing out the room and cleaning, or if you are leaving the house and closing it for a long time.

INGREDIENTS
- 1 ounce of witch hazel
- 2 ounces of distilled water
- 10 drops of lavender
- Bottle of room spray

PREPARATION

Making this room spray is very simple and easy. All you have to do is to mix the ingredients and shake well.

USAGE TIPS

This air freshener can be kept near entrance closets, where coats are held and where you keep shoes that may have a stale odor. Sometimes, it is necessary to spray this spray for an instant breath of freshness and cleanliness, even near the toilet or in the car's glove compartment.

6 - POWDERED LAUNDRY SOAP

Homemade laundry detergent isn't just for saving money, although it definitely is a smart economical move. But, these days, something is exciting about producing something you need. This powdered laundry soap allows you to be eco-friendlier, not impact the environment with harmful substances, and still clean smelly laundry.

INGREDIENTS
- 4 cups of borax
- 6 cups of baking soda
- 2 bars of Lavender Castille soap
- 20 drops of lavender essential oil

TOOLS
- Food processor
- Measuring cup
- Gloves
- Mask
- Large mixing spoon
- Container to hold the finished detergent
- Measuring cup for dosing the detergent

PREPARATION
First, you need to grind the soap, put it in the food processor, or grate it with a grater. Using the food processor's blades, keep grating the soap. Put borax baking soda, and the crushed soap in a large bowl, and mix with a whisk. Use gloves and a mask to avoid breathing in the vapors. Insert the 20 drops of lavender essential oil and store in an airtight container.

USAGE TIPS
You can use 1-2 scoops per load. We advise adding vinegar to the rinse for softer clothes and shake the contents of the jar from time to time to redistribute the components.

7 - LIQUID FLOOR CLEANER

Having a clean and delicately scented environment allows you to live better and more healthily. Preparing a lavender liquid detergent means sanitizing your home without using products that are harmful to your health and damaging to wooden floors and furniture made of delicate materials. If you need to wash often because you live with young children or pets, lavender is a natural ally.

INGREDIENTS
- 4 cups of white wine vinegar
- 2 cups of dried lavender flowers
- 1 glass of water
- 5 drops of lavender essential oil

PREPARATION
Take a 50.7 oz. glass bottle, use a funnel to pour dried lavender flowers into it, and then, add 4 cups of vinegar after heating it for 5-10 minutes. Close the bottle and place it in a warm and sunny place. Let the substance rest for about two weeks, making sure to shake it every day. Then, transfer the bottle's content into a clean nebulizer by filtering it through a linen cloth, adding a glass of water, and 5 drops of essential oil.

USAGE TIPS
This degreaser is excellent for cleaning any surface, especially glass and floors. It cleans thoroughly, leaving a wonderful lavender smell throughout the house. It also means having a suitable environment to combat stress and anxiety thanks to the calming power of this beautiful flower.

NATURAL PET PRODUCTS

1 - GEL FOR BITES AND INSECT STINGS

A dog is man's most trusted friend. They need all the possible attention that an owner can give them because they only reserve love for their family. Hence why it must be reciprocated.

Therefore, protecting them from bites and insect bites not only preserves them from annoying itches but also from diseases.

INGREDIENTS
- 1 ounce of aloe vera gel
- 5 drops of lavender Angustifolia essential oil
- 2 drops of helichrysum

PREPARATION
Take a large bottle with a darkened glass to protect the preparation from sunlight. Place the aloe gel inside, along with the essential oil drops, and then shake gently until the ingredients are perfectly blended. Leave to rest for an hour.

USAGE TIPS
This gel is perfect for treating insect bites and stings and relieving redness and itching. It has anti-inflammatory properties and helps heal the skin, preventing the appearance of infections thanks to the antibacterial properties of lavender.

Thanks to its composition, it can also be used to:
1. Prevent infections and help scratches and light wounds heal.
2. Drive away insects that are harmful to the dog's health through the smell.
3. Quickly sanitize your four-legged friend's skin.

2 - FLEA COLLAR FOR DOGS AND CATS

Fleas are very annoying pests, both for dogs and cats. They cause itching, and in some cases, can also lead to localized alopecia and infections.

In addition, your dog may scratch their wounds so much that it makes them impossible to heal without breeding ground for bacteria and fungi causing serious infections.

INGREDIENTS
- A cloth collar
- 3 drops of lavender essential oil
- 3 drops of lemongrass essential oil
- 1 tablespoon of alcohol
- 1 drop of garlic essential oil
- 1 drop of thyme essential oil

PREPARATION

Take a large bowl, add essential oils and a tablespoon of alcohol, and mix to allow the substances to combine perfectly. Next, take the cloth collar and immerse it completely in the mixture, leaving it for a few minutes until completely absorbed and dry.

USAGE TIPS

The lavender mixture prepared in this way can be used for two different purposes: to prepare a 100% natural and effective flea collar and to sanitize and repel fleas from pet kennels. It is recommended to prepare some more after about a month or when you realize that the essence has completely evaporated.

3 –DEODORANT

It is possible to reduce your pets' odors without using chemicals that can be harmful to the health of their skin and coat. When the coat has a strong odor despite grooming, it can sometimes be indispensable to take care of the house and the environment by giving your dog or cat a fresh and natural smell without causing him unnecessary stress.

INGREDIENTS
- 15 drops of lavender
- 2 tablespoons of vegetable glycerin
- 15 drops of sweet orange essential oil
- 1 tablespoon of coconut oil
- 2 cups of distilled water
- 1 fairly large spray bottle

PREPARATION
Take the spray bottle and fill it with two cups of distilled water. Add coconut oil and vegetable glycerin, along with essential oil drops. Shake vigorously to allow the ingredients to come together.

USAGE TIPS
Before using this deodorant spray, it is advisable to shake it. The lavender mixture, aided by the other oils, should be sprayed onto the dog or cat's coat in the right amount. Then, you should comb your pet with a brush to help the mixture penetrate deeply into their coat. This product will last for up to nine months if properly stored away from heat, humidity, and intense sunlight.

4 - DEODORIZER FOR LITTER BOX

When you have a cat in the apartment or kittens that cannot go out in the garden, the litter box is indispensable. However, sometimes, it is not enough to put it in an airy place to prevent the strong odors from spreading throughout the house. That is why a natural deodorizer that does not disturb the cat's health but prevents bad odors is indispensable.

INGREDIENTS
- 10 drops of lavender essential oil
- 1 jar full of baking soda

PREPARATION
Take a glass kitchen jar, fill it with baking soda, and then, pour over the drops of lavender essential oil. Shake well, using a teaspoon if necessary. Hermetically close the jar to prevent the dispersion of the essence.

Lavender oil is very suitable for perfuming the litter box without irritating the cat's skin. This scented salt can be sprinkled once a week, or as needed, directly into the litter box. We advise you to start with small doses and then increase them once the kitten has adapted to the new smell. Keep the jar in a dry place and away from sunlight to prevent moisture from ruining the product.

5 - SHAMPOO

Dog shampoos can be aggressive to their skin and hair. If you need to constantly keep your four-legged friend fresh and clean, you can resort to lavender and its properties, activated by the ingredients of this particular detergent. So, it possible to keep your dog clean and smelling fresh without using chemical agents.

INGREDIENTS
- 9 drops of lavender essential oil
- 2 tablespoons of castile soap
- 1 tablespoon of coconut oil
- ½ cup of baking soda
- ½ cup of distilled water
- ½ cup of oatmeal

PREPARATION
Take a blender and combine all the ingredients one by one, and then blend them. You must keep mixing until all the ingredients are combined into one uniform mixture. If there are any adhesions to the edges and between the blades, you can turn off the blender and use a teaspoon to stir everything together. Once you obtain the desired texture, place the mixture in an airtight jar and store it in the refrigerator.

USAGE TIPS
Take the jar out of the fridge a quarter of an hour before bathing the dog. Pick up a little solid shampoo with your fingers and rub the dog, making sure to cover the whole body and passing your fingers through the hair. Leave on for some time so that the soothing properties of oats and coconut oil untangle the hair and moisturize the skin.

At the same time, the castile soap and baking soda will have time to thoroughly disinfect, and the lavender will be able to provide a relaxing scent.

6 - PET SPRAYS

Whether a dog or a cat, a pet truly fills a life. Loving them unconditionally is the one thing an owner must do while caring for him.
Using only natural elements to combat their unpleasant odors without causing them discomfort with lavender is a breeze.

INGREDIENTS
- 15 drops of lavender essential oil
- 8.4 ounces of distilled water
- 1 spray bottle

PREPARATION
Take a spray bottle and fill it with 8.4 oz. of distilled water. Then, insert the drops of lavender essential oil and shake lightly to mix everything without creating foam or bubbles.

USAGE TIPS
Lavender has significant therapeutic and calming properties, and this spray can be used to:

1. Scent the dog's skin and coat without chemicals.
2. Eliminate parasites and bacteria.
3. Calm and relax the animal, given occasions where there will be guests in the house. Spraying a cloud 10-15 minutes before their arrival will allow you to calm the animal.

7 - NATURAL TOYS CLEANING

Our animal friends are always super pampered and need toys to both interact with their owners and play independently. It is essential to take care of these objects and disinfect them, especially in houses with children. Lavender is an effective antibacterial that comes to our aid, even in these most particular needs.

INGREDIENTS
- 2 ounces of liquid soap
- 5 drops of lavender essential oil
- Warm distilled water
- 24-ounce spray bottle

PREPARATION
The base of this cleaner for your pets' toys is liquid soap and distilled water: tap water is full of contaminants and bacteria and may contain fluoride or chlorine.
Finally, the essential oil fights germs and does not harm the animal, even if ingested, and is considered harmless, even for cats. To obtain the cleanser, you must mix the ingredients inside the spray bottle and shake slowly to avoid the creation of foam.

USAGE TIPS
Every time you use this spray, you must shake it a bit because the vegetable oils tend to separate. Once the toys have been cleaned, you have to rinse them with lukewarm water. This will have the dual effect of sanitizing the toys and eliminating any unpleasant odors that may lurk in the plastic.

8 - ANTI-ANXIETY SPRAYS FOR DOGS AND CATS

Many pets who live indoors can struggle with anxiety when left alone or when there are guests inside the apartment.
For our four-legged friends, experiencing too much stress is not nice and an owner can help them feel better by using the unique properties of lavender.

INGREDIENTS
- 2 cups of water
- 3 tablespoons of dried lavender flowers
- 1 cup of olive oil
- 3 drops of vetiver essential oil
- 3 drops of lavender essential oil
- 1 atomizer

PREPARATION

Take a glass jar and place 3 tablespoons of dried lavender flowers inside. Pour one cup of oil on top of the flowers. Place the jar inside a pot and fill it until the water fills half of the jar. Place it on the stove on low heat for about 3 hours. Let the oil cool, and then, filter it through a tightly woven linen cloth. Once this is done, squeeze the flowers left in the jar to let all the essence come out and add it to the filtered liquid. Take the nebulizer, fill it with 2 cups of water, and mix with the essence prepared in a bain-marie. Finally, add the drops of essential oils and stir.

USAGE TIPS

This preparation uses the calming properties of lavender and adds those of vetiver to create a powerful ally against our four-legged friends' anxieties. To use it efficiently, you can spray the product on the pet's coat 15 minutes before leaving the house to take them for a walk or going to work. This will:

- Make them better able to endure a car ride;
- Keep them calm before going to the vet;
- Make them feel more peaceful before guests arrive at your home.

NOTES

NOTES

DEMETER GUIDES

- To know us a little more -
Environmental awareness is important to us.
This book is printed-on-demand to reduce excess production.
The ink is chlorine-free, and the acid-free interior paper stock is provided by a supplier certified by the Forest Stewardship Council.
We chose to print in black and white on a cream-colored paper made with 30% post-consumer recycled material.
We believe you appreciate and share our choices.
Thank you so much for choosing us!
We trust that you, together with us, will continue to revise your daily practices to make sure we are doing our part to protect the environment.

- Your happiness matters to us! -
Have you bought the paperback version and are you wondering about color images?!
Visit us on Instagram @demeter_guides, and you will find the most beautiful and useful images published.

- To know you a little more -
Did you like this book? Did you find it interesting and useful?
We are always looking for ways to improve.
Our goal is to create the best content for you!
We would love to hear your feedback, and we would be incredibly grateful if you could take a couple of minutes to write a quick review for us.
You would help us improve and make known the value we provide.
Thank you! :)

Requests, ideas, any passionate suggestions?!
Contact us at demeterguides@gmail.com

See you soon and in the meantime...
...We wish you a wonderful life!

Demeter Guides

Made in the USA
Middletown, DE
03 September 2021